THE ILLUSTRATED DICTIONARY OF

PREHISTORIC LIFE

Copyright © 1993 Merlion Publishing Ltd
First published 1993 by
Merlion Publishing Ltd
2 Bellinger Close
Greenways Business Park
Chippenham
Wiltshire SN15 1BN
UK

Series editor: Merilyn Holme
Editor: Josephine Paker

Design: Jane Brett
Illustrations: Joanne Cowne; Jeremy Gower (B.L. Kearley Ltd);
Alan Male and Phil Weare (Linden Artists Ltd); Maltings
Partnership; Jamie Medlin; David Eddington (Maggie Mundy
Illustrators' Agency); Oxford Illustrators; Tony Morris (Linda Rogers
Associates); Peter Geissler (Specs Art Agency); Tony Gibbons
(Bernard Thornton Artists)
Cover illustration: Jeremy Gower (B.L. Kearley Ltd)

Consultant: Liz Cook BSc, Postgraduate
Researcher, Department of Geology, University of Bristol

Printed in Great Britain by BPCC Paulton Books Ltd

ISBN 1 85737 018 X

THE ILLUSTRATED DICTIONARY OF
PREHISTORIC LIFE

Contributors
Martin Walters
Josephine Paker

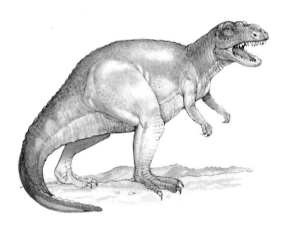

Merlion Publishing

Reader's notes

The entries in this dictionary have several features to help you understand more about the word you are looking up.

- Each entry is introduced by its headword. All the headwords in the dictionary are arranged in alphabetical order.

- Each headword is followed by a part of speech to show whether the word is used as a noun, adjective, verb or prefix.

- Each entry begins with a sentence that uses the headword as its subject.

- Words that are bold in an entry are cross references. You can look them up in this dictionary to find out more information about the topic.

- Words in italics in an entry are the scientific names of a genus or species of animal or plant.

- Many of the entries are illustrated. The labels on the illustrations highlight all the key points of information.

- Many of the labels on the illustrations have their own entries in the dictionary and can therefore be used as cross references.

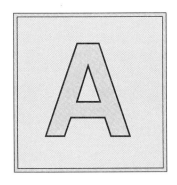

aboriginal *adjective*
Aboriginal describes an animal or plant which is native to an area of land. The aboriginal flora or fauna of a continent is that which **evolved** there. Lemurs are part of the aboriginal fauna of Madagascar.
aborigine *noun*

Abrictosaurus ▶ heterodontosaur

absolute dating *noun*
Absolute dating is a method of finding out the age of a **fossil** or **rock**. It measures the amount of decay of a radioactive chemical in the specimen. The amount of decay depends on the time which has passed since the fossil or rock formed. **Carbon dating** is one type of absolute dating.

Acanthopholis *noun*
Acanthopholis was a **dinosaur** which lived in the **Cretaceous Period**. It was a kind of **ankylosaur**. *Acanthopholis* was about 5.5 metres long, with a narrow head. Its body was covered in bony plates and spines. The first fossilized bones of *Acanthopholis* were found in southern England, in 1864. Only a few bones have been found since then, so little is known about *Acanthopholis*.

actinopterygian *noun*
Actinopterygians are a group of bony **fish**. They are the ray-finned fish. They have fleshy fins, stiffened by spines or rays. Most living bony fish belong to this group. The actinopterygians appeared in the **Devonian Period**. The other main group of fish is the **sarcopterygians**.

Aegyptopithecus *noun*
Aegyptopithecus was a kind of ape. It lived in the **Oligocene Epoch**. Fossils of this kind of ape have been found in Africa. *Aegyptopithecus* probably lived in a forest habitat.

Aepyornis *noun*
Aepyornis was a large bird. It lived in the **Quaternary Period**, and died out, or became extinct, about 10,000 years ago. Its fossilized bones and eggs have been found in Madagascar. It reached about three metres in length. *Aepyornis* is known as the elephant bird. It was the heaviest bird ever to have lived.

agnathan *noun*
An agnathan is one of a group of **fish**. The agnathans have no true jaws, but their mouthparts are formed from gills. They are the jawless fish. The agnathans were the earliest fish to evolve. They flourished in the **Silurian** and **Devonian Periods**. The lampreys and hagfish are living agnathans.

Agnostus *noun*
Agnostus was a **trilobite**. It lived in the **Cambrian** and **Ordovician Periods**. Fossils of *Agnostus* are found in many different parts of the world. They are known as **index fossils**, because they can be used to date rocks. *Agnostus* was only about five to ten millimetres long, and blind. It probably lived on the ocean floor.

Albertosaurus *noun*

Albertosaurus was a **dinosaur** which lived in the **Cretaceous Period**. It belonged to the **carnosaurs** and fed on meat. Skeletons of *Albertosaurus* have been found in North America. It is named after the province of Alberta, in Canada. *Albertosaurus* was about nine metres in length and had a large head, long tail and very short front legs. It ran about on its long, powerful back legs.

alga (plural **algae**) *noun*

An alga is a simple plant, which grows mostly in the water. There are about 25,000 species of alga. They grow in all parts of the world, especially in the sea, in lakes and in ponds. Seaweeds are algae, but many algae are tiny and can only be seen well with a microscope. The largest algae of all are kelp, which are found in shallow seas and can grow to hundreds of metres long. The algae appeared very early, as long ago as the **Precambrian Period**.

alligator *noun*

An alligator is a **reptile**. There are two species of alligator alive today. One is found in the United States of America, the other is found in China. American alligators are larger, reaching a length of 3.7 metres. Both species live in freshwater swamps and rivers and feed on birds, mammals and fish. The ancestors of alligators and crocodiles first appeared towards the end of the **Triassic Period**.

Allodesmus *noun*

Allodesmus was a marine **mammal**. It was related to fur seals. *Allodesmus* lived in the **Miocene Epoch**. Like the fur seals, the male *Allodesmus* was much larger than the female. They probably lived in colonies.

Allosaurus *noun*

Allosaurus was a **dinosaur** which lived in the late **Jurassic Period**. It belonged to the **carnosaurs** and fed on meat. *Allosaurus* was common in North America and has also been found in Africa and Australia. It reached a length of around 11 metres.

Alticamelus *noun*

Alticamelus was a relative of the camel. It lived about 20 million years ago, in the **Miocene Epoch**. *Alticamelus* had a long neck, rather like a giraffe. Fossils of *Alticamelus* have been found in North America.

amber *noun*

Amber is a shiny, orange or yellow mineral. It is formed from very old deposits of pine tree sap, or resin. Insects and other invertebrates are sometimes preserved in amber.

Amblotherium *noun*

Amblotherium was a small **mammal** which lived in the **Jurassic Period**. It grew to about 25 centimetres long and looked like a rodent, with a long tail. *Amblotherium* was **insectivorous** and its fossils have been found in Europe and North America.

amino acid *noun*
An amino acid is a kind of chemical mixture, or compound. Amino acids are the compounds from which proteins are made. Many scientists think that the earliest forms of life developed from amino acids, in the sea.

ammonite *noun*
An ammonite is an extinct kind of **mollusc**, related to squids and octopuses. Ammonites first appeared in the seas about 380 million years ago. They became extinct about 65 million years ago. Ammonites had a hard, chalky, spiral shell. These shells are preserved in some rocks as **fossils**.

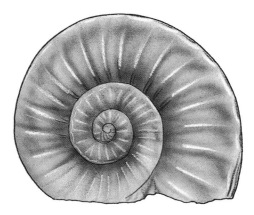

amphibian ► page 8

amphibious *adjective*
Amphibious describes an animal which lives in and out of the water. Many prehistoric animals were amphibious, as well as the **amphibians** themselves. An amphibious reptile was *Nothosaurus*.

anapsid *noun*
The anapsids are a group of **reptiles**. Turtles and tortoises belong to this group. The anapsids **evolved** during the **Triassic Period**. Anapsids are all plant-eaters, or **herbivores**. Some spend all their time on land and others are amphibious. Living anapsids have changed very little from their ancestors. There are three other groups of reptiles. These are the **diapsids**, the **euryapsids** and the **synapsids**.

Anatosaurus *noun*
Anatosaurus was a **dinosaur** which lived in the **Cretaceous Period**. It is known as a duck-billed dinosaur because it had a flattened head with a broad snout. *Anatosaurus* belonged to the **hadrosaurs** and fed on plants. It had webbed front feet, which may have helped it swim. But some scientists believe *Anatosaurus* only lived on land. *Anatosaurus* was a large animal, which could reach up to 13 metres in length.

Anchisaurus *noun*
Anchisaurus was a **dinosaur** which lived in the early **Jurassic Period**. It is known to have lived in North America and South Africa. It was one of the first dinosaurs to be discovered in America, a specimen being found in 1818. *Anchisaurus* belonged to the **prosauropod** group. It was a small animal, reaching about 2.5 metres long, and walked on its four short legs.

Andrewsarchus *noun*
Andrewsarchus was a large, bear-like mammal which lived in the **Eocene** and **Oligocene Epochs**. It was a fierce **carnivore**, feeding on other mammals of the grasslands of Mongolia. *Andrewsarchus* had a huge skull, with large teeth for crushing bones. It may have eaten plants as well as other animals.

angiosperm *noun*
An angiosperm is a flowering **plant**. There are about 250,000 species of angiosperm. They include all familiar flowers. Angiosperms also include most **trees**, except the **conifers**. They are divided into two sub-classes, the monocotyledons and the dicotyledons. When they start to grow, the seeds of monocotyledons produce a single leaf, or cotyledon. Dicotyledons produce two leaves. About two-thirds of all angiosperms live in the tropics. The angiosperms first evolved during the **Cretaceous Period**.

amphibian *noun*

An amphibian is a **vertebrate** animal that lives near water. Most amphibians lay eggs in the water, and spend the early part of their life in water. They evolved from **lobe-finned fish**. Amphibians were the first vertebrates to walk on land, and first appeared during the **Devonian Period**, about 380 million years ago.

Megalocephalus was a large early amphibian about two metres long. It lived in the swamps of the late Carboniferous Period. All that has been found of *Megalocephalus* is its crocodile-like skull.

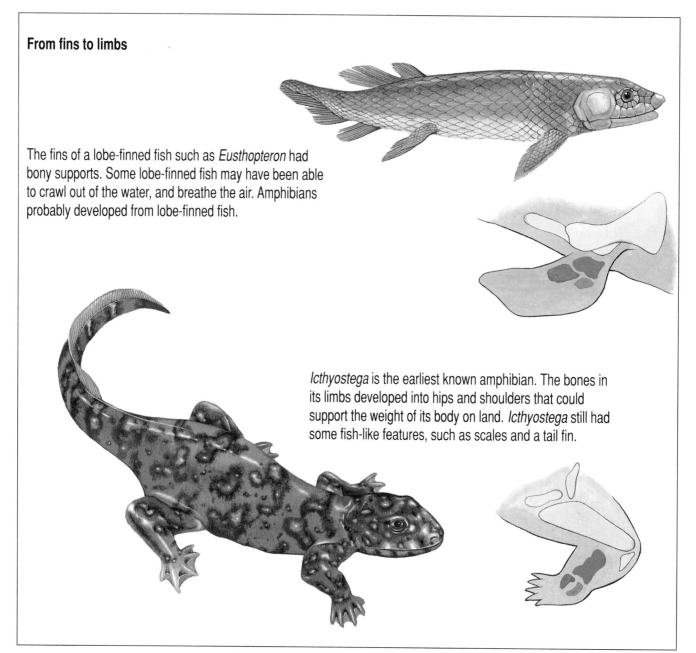

From fins to limbs

The fins of a lobe-finned fish such as *Eusthopteron* had bony supports. Some lobe-finned fish may have been able to crawl out of the water, and breathe the air. Amphibians probably developed from lobe-finned fish.

Icthyostega is the earliest known amphibian. The bones in its limbs developed into hips and shoulders that could support the weight of its body on land. *Icthyostega* still had some fish-like features, such as scales and a tail fin.

Eryops was a crocodile-like amphibian. It lived in the Permian Period. Its sharp teeth show that it was a meat eater. Paleontologists think *Eryops* had thick, tough skin, and lived in dry desert, though probably returned to the water to lay its eggs.

Eogyrinus was about four metres long. It lived in the Carboniferous Period, and probably fed on fish and other animals.

Diplocaulus had an unusual method of protecting itself. The flat, bony, boomerang-shaped plates on its head would have made it difficult for larger animals to eat it. These plates may also have helped *Diplocaulus* to swim.

Diadectes was well adapted to life out of water. It was a heavily built amphibian with powerful legs. Other amphibians of the time had sharp teeth for eating animals and insects. But the teeth of *Diadectes* were blunt, which shows that it may have been the first plant-eating amphibian.

animal *noun*

An animal is a living thing, or **organism**. Animals make up one of the five kingdoms of living things. Animals can move and respond to the world around them. There are over one million species of animal alive today. There are two main types of animal. The **vertebrates** are all the animals that have a **backbone**. The **invertebrates** are those animals without a backbone. Invertebrate animals first appeared in the **Precambrian Period**. The first vertebrate animals to evolve were the fish, in the **Cambrian Period**.

ankylosaur *noun*

An ankylosaur was one of a group of **dinosaurs** which lived mainly in the **Cretaceous Period**. Ankylosaurs fed on plants. They walked on all fours, with short, thick legs. Their body was heavily armoured with hard, bony plates and spikes. Some species of ankylosaur, such as *Euoplocephalus*, also had clubs or spikes at the end of their tail.

Ankylosaurus *noun*

Ankylosaurus was the biggest of the **ankylosaurs**. It lived in the **Cretaceous Period**, in North America. *Ankylosaurus* looked rather like a giant armadillo. It had bony spikes on its back, and a large, heavy club on the end of its tail. *Ankylosaurus* could swing this club and hit any predator which came too close. It grew to about 11 metres in length.

annelid *noun*

An annelid is a kind of **worm**. Annelids are also known as segmented worms, because their body is ringed. Earthworms, leeches and ragworms are all annelids. The earliest annelids evolved in the **Precambrian Period**. Because they are soft-bodied animals, very few of their **fossils** remain.

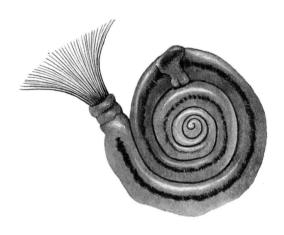

Annularia *noun*

Annularia is a fossil **horsetail**. It grew in the late **Carboniferous Period** and early **Permian Period**. *Annularia* had a stem filled with pith, and rosettes of leaves.

ant *noun*

Ants are small **insects**. There are about 10,000 species of ant living today. They range in size from 0.1 centimetre long to 2.5 centimetres long. Ants live in colonies, often in underground tunnels and galleries. They carry food over long distances. The first ants probably evolved in the **Devonian** and **Carboniferous Periods**. Insects such as ants are sometimes preserved in **amber**.

Antarctosaurus *noun*

Antarctosaurus was a large **dinosaur** from the **Cretaceous Period**. It belonged to the **sauropod** group. Most fossils of *Antarctosaurus* have come from South America. It had a long neck with a small head, and a long tail. *Antarctosaurus* fed on leaves, which it probably swallowed whole. It reached about 18 metres in length.

Anthracotherium   *noun*
Anthracotherium was a pig-like **mammal**. It lived in the **Miocene Epoch**, in tropical Africa and Asia. *Anthracotherium* may have been **amphibious**, like a hippopotamus.

Apatosaurus   *noun*
Apatosaurus was a large **dinosaur** from the **Jurassic Period**. It fed on plants like other members of the **sauropod** group. *Apatosaurus* grew to over 21 metres long, and probably weighed about 30 tonnes. It is also sometimes called *Brontosaurus*.

aquatic   *adjective*
Aquatic describes a **plant** or **animal** which lives in the water. The earliest forms of animal life were aquatic. Aquatic animals and plants began to evolve into land-living forms in the **Devonian** and **Carboniferous Periods**.

aquatic reptile ► page 12

Archaeopteryx   *noun*
Archaeopteryx is the earliest known **bird**. It dates from the **Jurassic Period** and was discovered in Germany. It was probably one of the first birds to fly. As an early bird, *Archaeopteryx* had many reptile features, such as bony teeth, a bony tail, and claws on its wings. But it also had feathered wings and probably flew quite well over short distances. *Archaeopteryx* was about 35 centimetres long.

Archaeotherium   *noun*
Archaeotherium was an early form of pig. It lived in the **Oligocene Epoch** and its fossils have been discovered in North America and Asia. Like many pigs, *Archaeotherium* had tusks and a long skull. It fed by digging in the soil for roots.

Archaeothyris   *noun*
Archaeothyris was a mammal-like reptile, or **therosaur**. It is the oldest of this group known and lived in the **Carboniferous Period**. It is the earliest ancestor of the mammals so far discovered. Its skeleton shows some features of reptiles, but also some of mammals. *Archaeothyris* had sharp teeth and fed on insects found on the forest floor.

Archean Eon   *noun*
The Archean Eon is the earliest period in the Earth's history. The Archean Eon lasted from the beginning of the Earth, about 4,600 million years ago, until about 2,500 million years ago. It forms the first part of the **Precambrian Period**. The earliest forms of life on Earth developed during the Archean Eon.

Archelon   *noun*
Archelon was a turtle which lived in the **Cretaceous Period**. Its skeletons have been found in North America. *Archelon* was very large, reaching a length of about four metres. It swam in a similar way to modern turtles, using flat, paddle-like front limbs to propel itself forwards.

11

aquatic reptile   *noun*

An aquatic reptile is a **reptile** that lives in the water. The earliest aquatic reptiles appeared during the **Permian Period**. During the Mesozoic Era, many different kinds of aquatic reptile evolved, and by the **Jurassic Period**, many of them had become an enormous size. Most aquatic reptiles became extinct at the same time as the dinosaurs at the end of the **Cretaceous Period**. Only the turtles survived.

2. *Icthyosaurus* looked rather like a modern dolphin. *Icthyosaurus* did not lay eggs, but gave birth to live young.

1. *Mesosaurus* had short limbs with paddle-like feet. Its sharp snout was lined with needle-like teeth.

3. *Mosasaurus* was a huge reptile, measuring 15 metres long. It had a long, flexible tail as well as wide flippers.

The shapes below show the size of each reptile compared with a man.

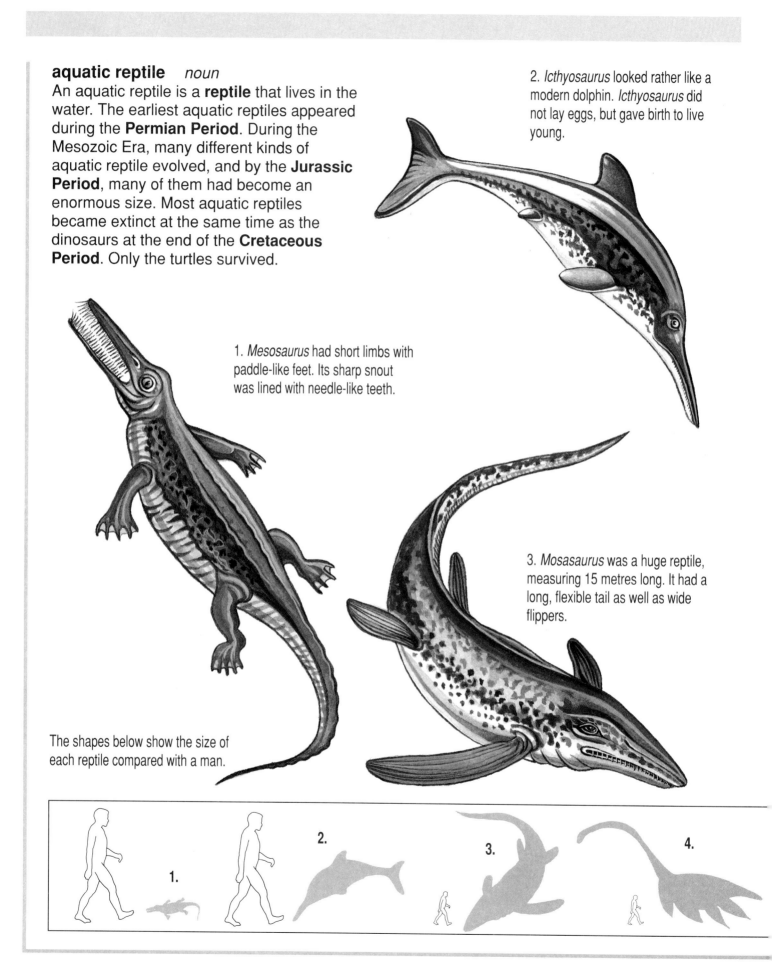

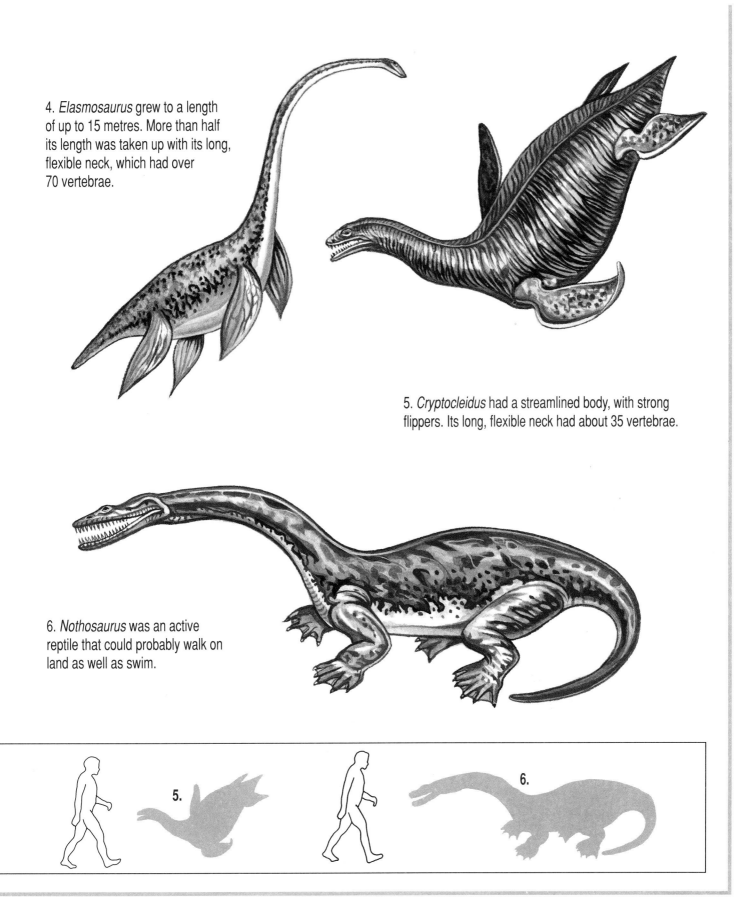

4. *Elasmosaurus* grew to a length of up to 15 metres. More than half its length was taken up with its long, flexible neck, which had over 70 vertebrae.

5. *Cryptocleidus* had a streamlined body, with strong flippers. Its long, flexible neck had about 35 vertebrae.

6. *Nothosaurus* was an active reptile that could probably walk on land as well as swim.

5.

6.

archosaur   *noun*
An archosaur was one of a large group of **reptiles**. Archosaurs included the **dinosaurs**, **pterosaurs** and **thecodonts**. The archosaur group also includes crocodiles.

Arctocyon   *noun*
Arctocyon was an early **mammal**. It lived in the early **Tertiary Period**. Fossils of *Arctocyon* have been found in North America and Europe. *Arctocyon* was small, with a fur-covered body and it had simple teeth.

Argentavis   *noun*
Argentavis was a huge bird which lived in North and South America in the **Miocene Epoch**. It was the largest flying bird known to have lived. Its wingspan was about seven metres.

Argyrolagus   *noun*
Argyrolagus was a **marsupial** which lived in South America during the **Pliocene Period**. It looked a little like a rabbit, with short arms, long hind legs and long teeth which were used for gnawing.

armoured dinosaur   *noun*
An armoured dinosaur was a **dinosaur** which had very thick skin with an armour of hard, bony plates, and studs and spikes which protected it from predators. There were three groups of armoured dinosaurs. These were the **ankylosaurs**, the **ceratopsians** and the **stegosaurs**.

Arsinoitherium   *noun*
Arsinoitherium was a **mammal** which lived in the **Oligocene Epoch**. Its fossil remains have been found in North Africa and the Middle East. It looked rather like a rhinoceros, with a thick body and two huge horns on its snout. *Arsinoitherium* grew to about three metres long. It probably lived in open country and fed by grazing on grasses and other low-growing plants.

arthropod   *noun*
An arthropod is an **invertebrate** animal. Arthropods make up the phylum arthropoda. They have jointed limbs and include insects, spiders and crustaceans. There are about one million different species of arthropod alive today. Arthropods first appeared in the **Cambrian Period**.

articulated   *adjective*
Articulated describes something that is joined in a way which allows movement. The neck **vertebrae** of many animals are articulated to allow movement and bending of the neck. The **sauropod** dinosaurs had a long, articulated neck.

artiodactyl   *noun*
An artiodactyl is a kind of **mammal** called an **ungulate**. It has an even number of toes on each foot. Artiodactyls include pigs, hippopotamuses, camels, deer, giraffes, goats and antelopes. They first appeared during the early **Eocene Epoch**, about 54 million years ago.

Askeptosaurus   *noun*
Askeptosaurus was a **reptile** which lived in the **Triassic Period**. It had a very long body, like a snake, and hands and feet like paddles. *Askeptosaurus* lived in the sea and probably swam by lashing its body from side to side. *Askeptosaurus* grew to about two metres long. Its long head was lined with sharp teeth for gripping its prey of slippery fish.

assemblage   *noun*
An assemblage is a group of **fossils**. Fossils belong to an assemblage if they are all found together in the same layer, or stratum, of rock. Fossils from a single assemblage usually lived at around the same time as each other.

Astrapotherium   *noun*
Astrapotherium was a **mammal** from South America. It lived in the **Oligocene** and **Miocene Epochs**. *Astrapotherium* had a long body and short legs. It was about three metres long and about one metre high. It probably had a flexible trunk like a tapir, and fed on forest shrubs and leaves.

aurochs   *noun*
An aurochs was a relative of today's cattle. Most farm cattle were probably domesticated from the aurochs, as long ago as 6500 BC. The aurochs lived in Asia, India and North Africa. They became extinct in the early 1600s.

Australopithecus   *noun*
Australopithecus was the oldest known **hominid**. It lived between 3 and 1.5 million years ago in the **Pliocene** and **Pleistocene Epochs**. Fossils of *Australopithecus* have been found in eastern and southern Africa. These early humans walked upright, as we do. But their brain was only the size of an ape's brain. *Australopithecus* lived by hunting small animals and gathering fruit and nuts.

autotrophic   *adjective*
Autotrophic describes a kind of feeding, or nutrition. Autotrophic organisms make their own food from simple chemicals. Green plants are autotrophic. They make their own food from carbon dioxide, using the energy of the Sun. The other main kind of feeding is **heterotrophic**.

Azoic Eon   *noun*
The Azoic Eon is one of the main divisions of geological history. It was the first eon and is the first part of the **Precambrian Period**. It is the part of the Earth's history before life evolved. The Azoic Eon is also known as the Priscoan Eon.

backbone *noun*
A backbone is part of an animal's **skeleton**.
Vertebrate animals all have backbones. The
backbone protects the spinal cord. It is made
up of many smaller bones, called **vertebrae**.
Backbones preserve well in rocks, and fossil
vertebrae are often discovered.

bacteria (singular **bacterium**) *noun*
Bacteria are tiny, one-celled living things, or
organisms. They are too small to be seen
without a microscope. Bacteria are found in
all habitats. Some live inside other plants
and animals, and cause diseases. Bacteria
were amongst the first kinds of life to evolve,
in the **Precambrian Period**.

Bagaceratops *noun*
Bagaceratops was a **dinosaur** which
belonged to a group called the
ceratopsians.

Baluchitherium *noun*
Baluchitherium was a large, odd-toed
ungulate. It lived in the **Oligocene Epoch** in
Asia. *Baluchitherium* was like a giant,
hornless rhinoceros. It was one of the
largest land **mammals** ever, standing nearly
5.5 metres high at the shoulder.
Baluchitherium is also known as
Indricotherium.

Barapasaurus *noun*
Barapasaurus was a dinosaur which lived in
the **Jurassic Period**. It was a **sauropod**.
Fossil remains of *Barapasaurus* have been
found in India, though no skulls have been
discovered so far.

Barbourofelis *noun*
Barbourofelis was a kind of large cat. It lived
in the **Miocene Epoch**, and its fossils have
been found in North America. It grew to
about 1.5 metres long. Like some other
extinct cats, *Barbourofelis* had a pair of long,
dagger-shaped upper teeth. It probably used
these to pierce the thick flesh of larger
animals such as elephants.

Barosaurus *noun*
Barosaurus was a large **dinosaur**. It
belonged to the **sauropod** group, and lived
in the **Jurassic Period**. Fossils of
Barosaurus have been found in Africa and in
North America. *Barosaurus* grew to a length
of about 25 metres. It had a long tail and a
very long neck.

Baryonyx *noun*
Baryonyx was a large, carnivorous dinosaur.
It belonged to the **carnosaur** group, and
lived in the **Cretaceous Period**. *Baryonyx*
had long, sharp claws and a flat head, rather
like a crocodile's. *Baryonyx* may have been
amphibious, and probably fed on fish. It
could grow to a length of nine metres.
Baryonyx was first discovered in 1983 when
fossils were dug from a claypit in Surrey,
England.

Basilosaurus *noun*
Basilosaurus was an early kind of whale.
It lived in shallow, warm seas, in the **Eocene
Epoch**. *Basilosaurus* had a fish-like tail,
short hind limbs and paddle-like front limbs.
It had sharp teeth and probably fed mainly
on fish.

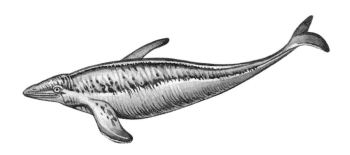

bat *noun*
A bat is a small, flying animal. It is the only **mammal** which can truly fly. There are about 980 species of bat. They live in all parts of the world, except towards the poles. The earliest fossil bat lived in the **Eocene Epoch**, but very few fossil bats have been discovered.

beak *noun*
A beak is part of a fossil. In **birds** and **cephalopods**, the beak is part of the jaw. In **bivalves**, the beak is part of the shell.

beaker people *noun*
The beaker people lived during the **Neolithic** Period, in parts of northern Europe. They were given this name because they made beakers out of pottery. The beaker people lived in huts containing simple rooms. They were **hunter-gatherers**, and also carried out simple farming.

bear *noun*
A bear is a large, stocky **mammal**. Most bears are **omnivores**, which means they eat meat as well as grass, fruit, leaves and nuts. There are seven species of bear. Bears evolved relatively recently, in the **Miocene Epoch**, about 20 million years ago.

bed *noun*
A bed is one particular layer, or stratum, in a sequence of rock strata. The **fossils** in one bed are usually of about the same age.

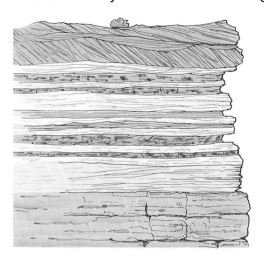

beetle *noun*
A beetle is a member of the largest of all the **insect** groups. There are more than 350,000 species of beetle alive today. They are found in all parts of the world except the oceans. Beetles are **omnivores** and feed on plants and animals. Fossil beetles have sometimes been found in **sandstone**. The earliest beetles that have been found date from the **Permian Period**.

belemnite *noun*
A belemnite is one of a group of extinct **molluscs**. Belemnites are related to the squids, cuttlefish and octopuses of today. Belemnites had a squid-shaped body, with tentacles on the head. They lived in the sea in the **Jurassic** and **Cretaceous Periods**. The part of a belemnite which is usually found fossilized is the **calcite** skeleton. This has a cylindrical shape and is also known as a pen, or guard.

fossilized belemnite

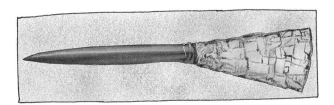

bennettite *noun*
A bennettite, or cycadeoid, was a palm-like plant. It belonged to the **gymnosperm** class. The bennettite's closest living relatives are the **cycads**. The bennettites flourished in the **Jurassic** and **Cretaceous Periods**, but did not survive until today. They had tough, leathery leaves and flower-like cones. *Williamsonia* was an example of a bennettite.

biologist *noun*
A biologist is someone who studies or practises **biology**.

bird *noun*

A bird is an animal that has wings and feathers. Birds lay eggs with hard shells. Most scientists believe that birds evolved from one of the families of **carnivorous dinosaur**, such as *Coelophysis*. The first bird was *Archaeopteryx*. It dates from the late **Jurassic Period**, though **flying reptiles** had existed since the **Permian Period**. The bones of birds are light and delicate, so not many have been fossilized.

Compsognathus was a small, carnivorous dinosaur that lived in the late Jurassic Period. It was from 70 to 140 centimetres tall. The skeleton of *Compsognathus* is very like that of *Archaeopteryx*.

Archaeopteryx had feathers like modern birds. But it also had a scaly head, with teeth, claws on its wings, and a long, bony tail, like a reptile.

Icthyornis looked rather like a seagull. It probably swooped low over the water, then dived to grab fish in its toothed beak.

Wings for flying

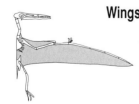

A pterosaur's wing was supported by one elongated finger.

A bat's wing is stretched over four fingers.

Diatryma could probably run as fast as a modern ostrich. It could not fly, and had a sharp beak.

Hesperornis was a large diving bird with teeth. It was about two metres high.

Phorusrhacus was a giant, flightless bird that lived in the Miocene Period.

The Elephant bird stood over three metres high and weighed up to 450 kilograms.

A bird's wing is supported on the whole arm.

A gliding lemur does not really fly. It glides on the flap of skin stretched between its limbs.

biology *noun*
Biology is the study of living things, or **organisms**. There are two main branches of biology. Zoology is the study of animals, and botany is the study of plants. The study of fossil animals and plants is known as paleobiology or **paleontology**.

biped *noun*
A biped is an animal that normally walks on two legs. Several groups of dinosaurs, including the **carnosaurs**, **ornithopods** and **pachycephalosaurs**, were bipeds. Other biped animals are humans and birds.
bipedal *adjective*

bird ▶ page 18

bird-footed dinosaur ▶ ornithopod

bird-hipped dinosaur ▶ ornithischian

bison *noun*
A bison is a large, hoofed **mammal**. Bison first appeared about three million years ago, in the **Pliocene Epoch**. They are large **herbivores**, belonging to the cow family. Bison graze in large herds on grassland.

bivalve *noun*
A bivalve is a **mollusc**. Bivalves form one of the main mollusc classes. There are about 15,000 species of bivalve alive today. Bivalves have two shells, hinged together. Tiny bivalves first appeared in the lower **Cambrian Period**.

blue-green alga (plural **algae**) *noun*
Blue-green algae are tiny, one-celled **organisms**. They belong to the kingdom *Monera*, which includes **bacteria**. Blue-green algae were among the first organisms to evolve. Some of their **fossils** may be 3,500 million years old. Some blue-green algae left behind fossils known as **stromatolites**.

bone *noun*
Bone is a hard substance found in the bodies of **vertebrate** animals. Bones are made of calcium phosphate. The fossils of vertebrate animals are usually made up of mineralized bone. The flesh and fur normally rots away, leaving the bone behind.

bony fish ▶ osteichthian

Borhyaena *noun*
Borhyaena was a large **marsupial**. It lived in South America in the **Miocene Epoch**. *Borhyaena* had sharp teeth and chased and killed other mammals.

brachiopod *noun*
Brachiopods are a phylum of **invertebrate** animals. Only about 350 species are known today, but there are many **fossil** brachiopods. More than 3,000 different **genera** of fossil brachiopods have been discovered. In some types of **rock**, brachiopods are the most common fossils. Brachiopods have a pair of hard shells, rather like **bivalve** molluscs.

Brachiosaurus *noun*
Brachiosaurus was a large **dinosaur**. It lived in the **Jurassic Period**. Fossils of *Brachiosaurus* have been dug up in East Africa and in North America. *Brachiosaurus* was one of the largest dinosaurs known, growing to more than 22 metres long from head to tail and weighing about 86 to 102 tonnes. It had a massive body, with a long tail and long neck. *Brachiosaurus* probably fed mostly on leaves, browsing on soft water plants in the swamps and estuaries. It may have stretched its neck to feed on leaves at the top of trees, like a giraffe.

Brachyceratops *noun*
Brachyceratops was a small **dinosaur** which lived in the **Cretaceous Period**. It belonged to the **ceratopsian** group and was one of the short-frilled ceratopsids. *Brachyceratops* means 'short-horned face'. *Brachyceratops* had a large, slightly curved horn on its snout and smaller horns above its eyes. It had a large head and four short, sturdy legs. *Brachyceratops* was only about 1.8 metres long. Its remains have been found in North America.

Brachylophosaurus *noun*
Brachylophosaurus was a **dinosaur** which lived in the **Cretaceous Period**. It belonged to the group known as duck-billed dinosaurs, or **hadrosaurs**. On its head, *Brachylophosaurus* had a solid crest and a small spike that pointed backwards. A broad plate ran between its eyes. Bones of *Brachylophosaurus* have been found in North America.

brain *noun*
A brain is a part of an animal's body. It is the controlling part of the central nervous system. In most animals, the brain is in the head, protected by the skeleton. In **vertebrates**, it lies inside the skull. As humans evolved, they developed larger and larger brains.

Brontosaurus ► **Apatosaurus**

Brontotherium *noun*
Brontotherium was a large, herbivorous **mammal**. It lived in the **Oligocene Epoch**. *Brontotherium* stood about 2.5 metres high at the shoulder and looked rather like a rhinoceros. It had a Y-shaped horn on the top of its snout. *Brontotherium* fed on leaves, which it pulled from forest trees and bushes.

Bronze Age *noun*
The Bronze Age was a period in human history. It lasted from about 3500 BC to about 600 BC. In the Bronze Age, people first learned how to make the metal bronze by melting copper and tin together. They began to use tools made of bronze.

browser *noun*
A browser is a kind of **herbivorous** animal. Browsers feed by chewing off pieces of trees, bushes and other plants as they walk along. Many **mammals**, such as antelopes and horses, are browsers.
browse *verb*

bryozoan *noun*
A bryozoan, or moss animal, is a member of the **invertebrate** phylum *Bryozoa*. There are about 4,000 species of bryozoan alive today. Bryozoans live in colonies and have a hard skeleton. Some kinds of **limestone** are made up of millions of skeletons of fossil bryozoans.

Burgess Shale   *noun*
The Burgess Shale is the name of a rock formation found in Canada. The Burgess Shale is rich in **fossils**. Many of these fossils are of soft-bodied animals which have not been found anywhere else in the world. These are the oldest multi-celled animals known. The Burgess Shale dates from the **Cambrian Period**, making the fossils about 530 million years old. Over 40 different species of **arthropod** are known from the Burgess Shale, including **trilobites**.

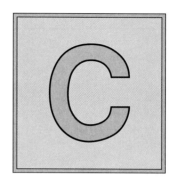

Calamites   *noun*
Calamites is an extinct **plant**. It is one of the most common of the fossil **horsetails**. *Calamites* had a woody, branched stem and grew to a height of about 20 metres. It lived in the **Devonian** and **Carboniferous Periods**.

calcite   *noun*
Calcite is a mineral. It is made up of crystals of calcium carbonate. Some animals, such as **echinoderms**, have calcite in their **skeleton**.

Camarasaurus   *noun*
Camarasaurus was a dinosaur which lived in the **Jurassic Period**. It was a **sauropod**, and was about 18 metres long. *Camarasaurus* had hollow spaces inside its vertebrae. These hollows helped to reduce the animal's weight.

Cambrian Period ▶ page 23

Camptosaurus   *noun*
Camptosaurus was a large **dinosaur**. It lived in the **Jurassic Period**. *Camptosaurus* was rather like *Iguanodon*, and walked mostly on its hind legs. It was about six metres long.

canine   *noun*
A canine is a kind of tooth. Canine teeth are long, curved and sharp. Animals use canines for biting and tearing flesh. **Carnivores** such as tigers and dogs have large canines. The canines belonging to the group of extinct sabre-toothed cats were extremely long.

Cambrian Period   *noun*

The Cambrian Period was a time in **geological history**. The Cambrian Period lasted from about 590 million years ago to about 505 million years ago. Many groups of **invertebrates** existed in the Cambrian Period. The only **vertebrates** in existence were **fish**. Nearly all life on Earth in the Cambrian Period existed in the sea. Many Cambrian fossils have been found in the **Burgess Shale**.

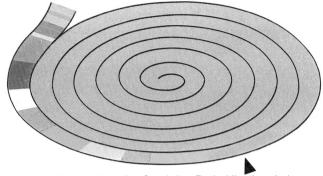

The arrow shows where the Cambrian Period lies in relation to the geological history of the Earth.

1. crinoids
2. shrimps
3. algae
4. vauxia sponge
5. *Hallucigenia*
6. trilobites

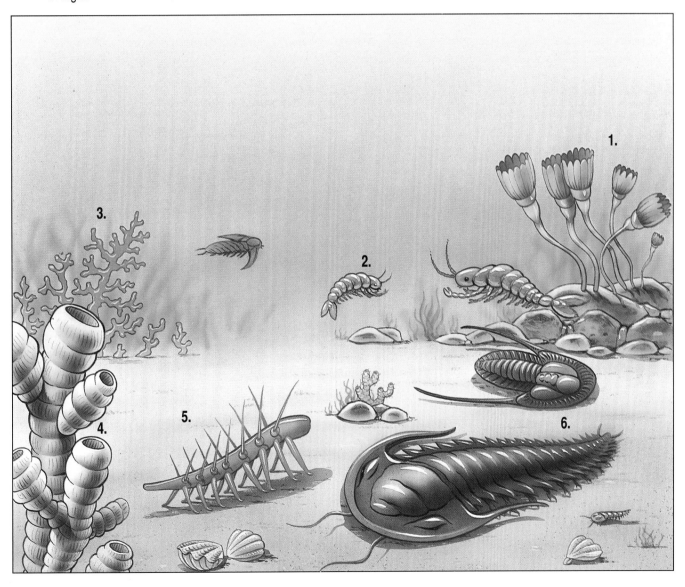

Carboniferous Period *noun*

The Carboniferous Period was a time in **geological history**. The Carboniferous Period lasted from about 360 million years ago to about 286 million years ago. **Reptiles** first appeared during the Carboniferous Period. Dead plants that grew in the swamps of the Carboniferous Period became compressed over millions of years to form the **coal** that is mined today.

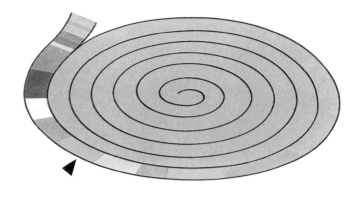

The arrow shows where the Carboniferous Period lies in relation to the geological history of the Earth.

1. *Mesosaurus*
2. *Edaphosaurus*
3. *Crassigyrinus*
4. *Stenodictya*
5. dragonfly

carapace *noun*
A carapace is the shell-like part of the hard **skeleton** covering the body of some animals. This kind of skeleton is called an exoskeleton. Crabs, lobsters and other **crustaceans** have a carapace. Some **vertebrates**, such as turtles and tortoises, also have a carapace.

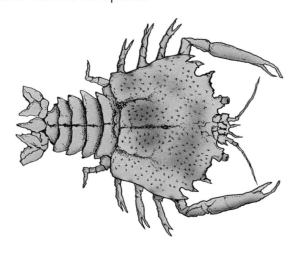

carbon dating *noun*
Carbon dating is a kind of **absolute dating**. It measures the **radioactivity** of a kind of carbon which all living things contain from the moment they were created. Carbon dating is used to measure the age of **fossils**.

Carboniferous Period ▶ page 24

Carcharodon *noun*
Carcharodon is an extinct kind of shark. It is the **genus** to which the great white shark belongs. This kind of shark first appeared in the **Cretaceous Period**. *Carcharodon* had large, triangular teeth with which it tore the flesh of its prey.

Carcharodontosaurus *noun*
Carcharodontosaurus was a large **dinosaur**. It belonged to the **carnosaur** group and fed on other animals. *Carcharodontosaurus* lived in the **Cretaceous Period** and its **fossilized** remains have been found in northern Africa. It grew to a length of about eight metres.

carnivore *noun*
A carnivore is an animal which eats other animals. The **carnosaurs** were carnivorous dinosaurs. Carnivores are also an order of **mammals**. They include cats, dogs, weasels, bears and hyenas.
carnivorous *adjective*

carnivorous dinosaur ▶ page 28

carnosaur *noun*
The carnosaurs were a group of **dinosaurs**. They all had a large body and fed by catching and killing other animals. Carnosaurs mostly lived in the **Jurassic** and **Cretaceous Periods**. The best known carnosaur is *Tyrannosaurus*. The carnosaurs had powerful jaws with large, sharp teeth.

cartilage *noun*
Cartilage is a strong tissue found in **vertebrate** animals. Cartilage is more flexible than **bone**. Sharks and related fish have a skeleton made of cartilage. The pads between the vertebrae of the backbone are made of cartilage.

cartilaginous fish ▶ **chondrichthian**

cast *noun*
A cast is a model of a fossil or bone. The first stage is to make a mould around the object. Then the mould can be filled with plaster. When the plaster sets, the cast is complete.

cave art ► page 30

cave bear   *noun*
A cave bear was a bear which is now extinct. It lived in Europe about 250,000 years ago. The bones of the cave bear have been found in many European caves. The cave bear was like the brown bear, but it had a higher forehead. It was about two metres long. Like many modern bears, cave bears probably hibernated during the cold winter months. They were omnivores, feeding on plants as well as other animals.

cave hyena   *noun*
A cave hyena was a **carnivore** which is now extinct. It lived in the **Pleistocene Epoch**, at the same time as the sabre-toothed cats, or **machairodonts**. The cave hyena was a powerful animal, nearly twice the size of today's hyenas. Many fossils of cave hyenas have been found in caves.

cave lion   *noun*
A cave lion was a carnivorous **mammal** and relative of the lion. It is now extinct. The cave lion lived in the **Pleistocene Epoch** and its remains have been found in many caves in Europe.

Cenozoic Era   *noun*
The Cenozoic Era is the most recent time in **geological history**. The Cenozoic Era began about 65 million years ago and continues to the present day. It is divided into two major periods. These are the **Tertiary Period** and the **Quaternary Period**. Most **mammals** have lived during the Cenozoic Era.

centipede   *noun*
A centipede is an **arthropod**. There are about 3,000 species of centipede alive today. Centipedes first appeared in the **Silurian Period**, but fossil centipedes are only rarely found.

Centrosaurus   *noun*
Centrosaurus was a **dinosaur** which lived in the **Cretaceous Period**. It was a medium-sized member of the **ceratopsian** group, and probably lived in large herds, **browsing** on plants. *Centrosaurus* had a single horn on its snout and small spines around its neck frill. It had four strong legs and small hooves on its feet. Fossils of *Centrosaurus* have been found in North America.

cephalopod   *noun*
A cephalopod is one of a group of **molluscs**. The cephalopods include octopuses, squids and cuttlefish. There are about 650 species of cephalopod alive today. The **nautiloids**, **ammonites** and **belemnites** also belong to this group. The earliest cephalopods date from the upper **Cambrian Period**.

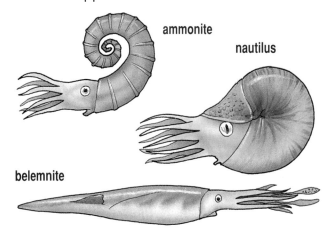

ammonite

nautilus

belemnite

ceratopsian   *noun*
A ceratopsian was one of a group of **dinosaurs**. Ceratopsians all had horns on their head and a thick, heavy body. The best known is *Triceratops*. The ceratopsians fed on leaves and other plants, and most walked on all fours. They lived during the **Cretaceous Period** and were some of the last dinosaurs to survive.

carnivorous dinosaur *noun*

A carnivorous dinosaur was a **dinosaur** that ate flesh. Many carnivorous dinosaurs belonged to the group called the carnosaurs. These were all large animals that killed their prey with sharp teeth and powerful jaws. Most of the carnosaurs lived in the **Jurassic** and **Cretaceous Periods**.

1. *Gallimimus* was a bird-like dinosaur which had a large, horny beak.

2. The jaws of *Allosaurus* were lined with sharp teeth with serrated edges.

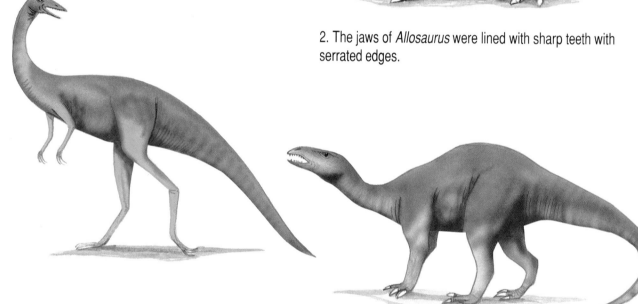

3. *Baryonyx* may have caught fish with its enormous hooked claws.

The shapes below show the size of each dinosaur compared with a man.

1.   2.   3.

4. *Tyrannosaurus* was the largest carnivore there has ever been.

5. *Coelophysis* was one of the most primitive dinosaurs. It was lightly-built and could probably run fast.

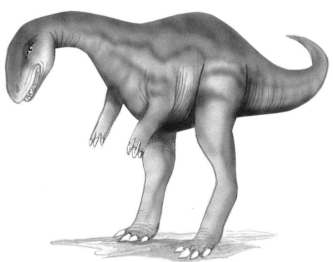

6. *Deinonychus* had a huge, sickle-shaped claw on the second toe of each foot. Its teeth curved backwards.

7. *Segnosaurus* may have fed on fish with its horny beak and small, pointed teeth. Incomplete skeletons of *Segnosaurus* have been found in Mongolia.

4.

5.

6.

7.

cave art   *noun*

Cave art describes the drawings and paintings made in caves by early people. Some **Paleolithic** people decorated the walls of their caves with paintings and drawings of the animals they hunted. Some of the most famous cave paintings are at Lascaux, France. They were painted between 17,000 and 15,000 years ago, at the end of the Old **Stone Age**. Cave art is specially interesting to **paleontologists**. It gives clues about extinct animals that cannot be guessed from a skeleton. For instance, it can show what an animal's coat was like.

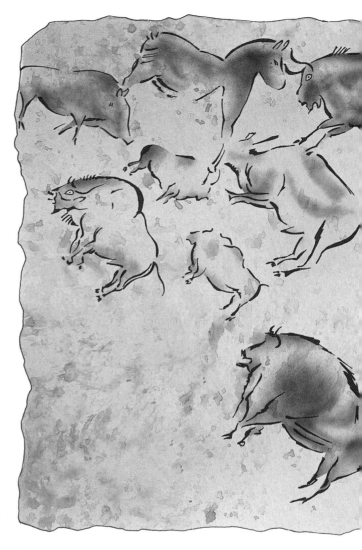

This shows part of a cave painting found in Altamira, Spain.

Paleolithic man used feathers or chewed twigs as paintbrushes. Colours for the paintings were ground from rock, clay, charcoal and earth. Pictures were also scratched into the rock with a sharp stone.

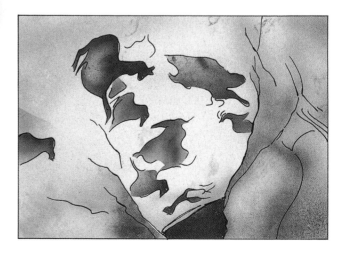

Bulls, horses and deer were painted all over the limestone ceilings at Lascaux, France.

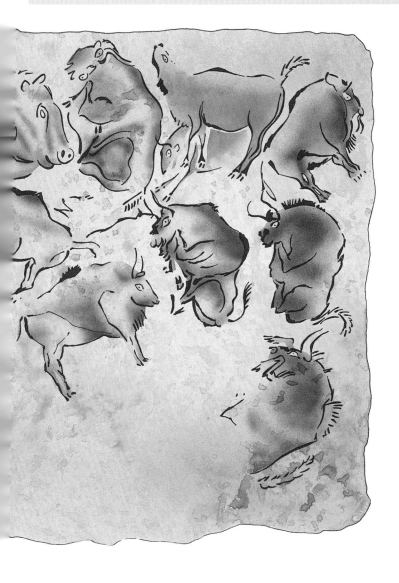

Cave paintings found in Tassili, Algeria, were made about 4,700 years ago.

This painting of a galloping pregnant horse at Lascaux gives a good sense of movement.

There is only one drawing of a human at Lascaux, France. It is a stick figure with a bird head.

Ceratosaurus   *noun*
Ceratosaurus was a **dinosaur** which lived in
the **Jurassic Period**. It belonged to the
carnosaur group and fed on meat.
Ceratosaurus had a horn on its nose. It grew
to about six metres long and had large,
sharp teeth. Its remains have been found in
North America and East Africa.

Cetiosaurus   *noun*
Cetiosaurus was a large **dinosaur**. It
belonged to the **sauropod** group. It was one
of the first dinosaurs to be discovered,
around 1840. *Cetiosaurus* grew to a length
of about 18 metres. Its skeletons have been
found in Europe and North Africa.

chalicothere   *noun*
A chalicothere was one of a family of hoofed
mammals. The chalicotheres lived from the
Eocene until the early **Pliocene Epochs**.
They belonged to the odd-toed **ungulates**,
which include rhinoceroses, tapirs and
horses. Chalicotheres were horse-sized
browsing animals, which probably ate
leaves and fruit.

Chalicotherium   *noun*
Chalicotherium was an early kind of odd-
toed **ungulate**. *Chalicotherium* and its
relatives lived from the **Eocene** to the
Pleistocene Epochs. Its front legs were
longer than its hind legs, which gave it an
odd, unbalanced look. *Chalicotherium* had
claws instead of hooves on its feet.

chalk   *noun*
Chalk is a kind of **limestone** rock. It is made
from the tiny shells of marine animals and is
often pure white. Chalk is mostly calcium
carbonate.

Champsosaurus   *noun*
Champsosaurus was an **amphibious**
dinosaur. It looked rather like a crocodile.
Champsosaurus lived in the **Cretaceous**
and early **Tertiary Periods**. It grew to about
1.5 metres long. *Champsosaurus* probably
swam well and hunted in the water for fish
and other animals. Its remains have been
found in Canada and France.

chelonian   *noun*
A chelonian is one of a group of **reptiles**.
These are the turtles, tortoises and
terrapins. Chelonians have a hard, box-like
shell. They can pull their limbs and head into
their shell for safety. Chelonians first
appeared, on land, in the upper **Triassic**
Period. Later forms took to the water. Some,
such as ***Archelon***, were very large.
chelonian   *adjective*

chondrichthian   *noun*
A chondrichthian is one of a group of **fish**.
The chondrichthians are the cartilaginous
fish, such as sharks, dogfish, rays and
rabbitfish. Their skeleton is made of
cartilage, not bone. There are about 700
species of chondrichthian alive today. They
first appeared in the **Devonian Period**, in
the sea.

chordate   *noun*
A chordate is one of a **phylum** of animals.
The most familiar chordates are the
vertebrates. They also include the lancelets
and the sea squirts. Chordates have a
hollow nerve cord, called the **notochord**.
The chordates first evolved in the upper
Cambrian Period.
chordate   *adjective*

class   *noun*
A class is part of the system of classification
of living things, or **organisms**. In animal
classification, each **phylum** contains one or
more classes. For example, the **mammals**
form a class within the **chordate** phylum,
and the **cephalopods** are a class within the
mollusc phylum.

claw   *noun*
A claw is a sharp nail on the foot of an
animal. Examples of animals which have
claws are birds, reptiles, many mammals
and amphibians, and also many insects and
crustaceans. Cats have claws which they
can draw in, or retract.

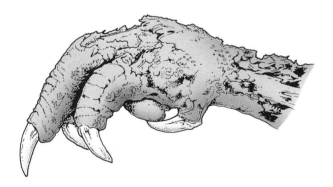

clay   *noun*
Clay is a mud-like substance that is formed
from tiny particles of minerals. Clay minerals
are made up mostly of sheets of silicates.
Clay cracks when dry. It takes in, or absorbs,
water easily, and becomes sticky and soft.
When dead animals become trapped in beds
of clay under water, they may turn into
fossils. Clay has been used by people for
making pots for thousands of years.

Clevosaurus   *noun*
Clevosaurus was a small **reptile** which lived
in the **Triassic Period**. It looked very similar
to the **tuatara** of today. *Clevosaurus* was
smaller, at 20 centimetres long. Its teeth
were different from the tuatara's and show
that it may have fed on plants as well as
insects. Well-preserved bones of
Clevosaurus have been found in caves in
southern England and Wales.

climate   *noun*
Climate is the overall weather of a site or
region. Temperature, rainfall, altitude and
distance from the sea all affect the climate.
Polar, temperate, oceanic and
Mediterranean are some of the major kinds
of climate. Countries close to the Equator
have a tropical climate.

club moss ► **lycopod**

coal   *noun*
Coal is a kind of **deposit** which is rich in
carbon. It forms when organic material, such
as the remains of plants, are crushed for
millions of years by layers of sedimentary
rock. Coal began to form in the
Carboniferous Period.

cockroach   *noun*
A cockroach is a kind of **insect**. There are
about 3,500 different species of cockroach.
They have a flattened body and long
antennae. Cockroaches are some of the
oldest kinds of insect. They first appeared
during the **Carboniferous Period**.

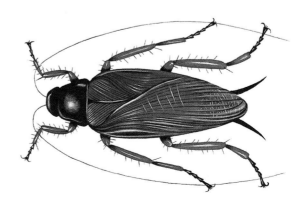

coelacanth *noun*
A coelacanth is a kind of bony fish. It belongs to a group called the **sarcopterygians**. These fish had fleshy fins, a little like limbs. They lived from the **Devonian Period** until the end of the **Cretaceous Period**. Most are known only from **fossils**, and the coelacanth was thought to be extinct. But then a live coelacanth was found in 1938, in the sea off south-east Africa. Other coelacanths have been found in the same sea since that time.

Coelodonta *noun*
Coelodonta was the woolly **rhinoceros**. It lived from the **Miocene Epoch** until the **Pleistocene Epoch**, in Europe and Asia. *Coelodonta* was about four metres long, with thick fur and humped shoulders. It had two horns in line on its snout. *Coelodonta* fed on grasses and shrubs. It was probably hunted by people, as it can be seen in cave paintings.

Coelophysis *noun*
Coelophysis was a dinosaur which lived in the **Triassic Period**. It belonged to the **coelurosaur** group. It had long, sturdy back legs and could probably run fast on these, as well as on all fours. Hundreds of well-preserved **fossils** of *Coelophysis* were found together in North America. *Coelophysis* fed on small animals by using its sharp teeth. It had a light skeleton and grew to a length of about three metres. *Coelophysis* was a **carnivore**.

coelurosaur *noun*
A coelurosaur was one of a group of **dinosaurs** from the **Triassic** and **Jurassic Periods**. The coelurosaurs had powerful jaws with sharp teeth and fed on meat. Most coelurosaurs walked and ran on their hind legs. This group includes dinosaurs such as *Coelophysis*, *Coelurus* and *Compsognathus*.

Coelurus *noun*
Coelurus was a dinosaur from the **Jurassic Period**. It was one of the smallest of the **coelurosaurs**, reaching a length of only about two metres. The remains of *Coelurus* have been found in North America.

cold-blooded *adjective*
Cold-blooded describes an animal which cannot adjust its own body temperature. Its temperature remains the same as that of its surroundings. Cold-blooded animals have to move into the shade if they are too hot, or bask in the Sun if they are too cold. Most animals are cold-blooded. Like living reptiles, **dinosaurs** were probably cold-blooded. The opposite of cold-blooded is **warm-blooded**.

Compsognathus *noun*
Compsognathus was a **dinosaur** from the **Jurassic Period**. It belonged to the **coelurosaur** group. At about 70 to 140 centimetres tall, it was even smaller than *Coelurus*. *Compsognathus* had long hind legs for running and a long, flexible neck and tail. Fossils of *Compsognathus* have been found in Europe.

condylarth *noun*
Condylarths were a group of **mammals**. They lived from the late **Cretaceous Period** until the **Miocene Epoch**. Condylarths were the ancestors of the **ungulates**. They had a long body and short legs. The feet of most condylarths had claws rather than the hooves of modern ungulates.

cone-bearing tree ► **conifer**

34

conifer *noun*
A conifer is a tree which develops cones. Conifers form part of the **gymnosperm** group. Pines, spruces and firs are conifers. Conifers mostly grow tall and straight. Their needle-shaped leaves are constantly replaced, not lost all at once. The conifers appeared in the **Carboniferous Period**, and were common in the **Jurassic Period**.
coniferous *adjective*

continent *noun*
A continent is a large land-mass on the Earth. There are now seven continents — Asia, Africa, North America, South America, Antarctica, Europe and Australia. Asia is the largest continent. In the past, the continents were joined together as **super-continents**.

continental drift *noun*
Continental drift describes how **continents** move, or drift, over the surface of the Earth. All the continents have gradually moved apart from one large land-mass, called **Pangaea**, by continental drift.

convergent evolution *noun*
Convergent evolution is a result of the **evolution** of animals. It happens when similar animals evolve in unrelated groups. Examples of convergent evolution are the mouse and the marsupial mouse. The marsupial mouse evolved separately from other mice, but it looks similar.

Cooksonia *noun*
Cooksonia is an extinct **plant**. It is the earliest known land plant, and belonged to the **pteridophyte** group. *Cooksonia* lived in the **Silurian** and **Devonian Periods**. It grew to about seven centimetres high and had stems with Y-shaped branches. *Cooksonia* reproduced by means of **spores**.

copper age *noun*
The copper age is the name given to a period of history in Europe, around 3000 BC. At this time, people first began to use metal, although stone was still also used for **tool-making**. They made tools and objects, such as knives, daggers and pins, by beating copper. They found the copper as **deposits** of ore either on the surface, or by mining.

coprolite *noun*
A coprolite is a kind of **trace fossil**. A coprolite is made of the fossilized droppings of animals. Most coprolites come from the droppings of fish or other marine animals. They contain the fossilized remains of food eaten by the animals.

coral *noun*
A coral is a kind of marine animal which has a hard **skeleton**. Corals are related to **sea anemones**. When some corals die, their hard, calcium carbonate skeletons build up to form coral reefs. Corals live in warm, shallow seas. Many fossil corals have been found, from as long ago as the **Ordovician Period**.

cordaitales *noun*
The cordaitales were a group of **plants** which lived in the **Carboniferous** and **Permian Periods**. They belonged to the **gymnosperm** group. The cordaitales were trees, with long leaves. They are thought to be the ancestors of the **conifers**.

Cordaites *noun*
Cordaites was a member of the **cordaitales** group. It lived in the **Carboniferous** and early **Permian Periods**, in many parts of the world. It grew in swampy ground. *Cordaites* reached a height of about 10 metres, and had long leaves, arranged in spirals.

craniate ► vertebrate

cranium *noun*
A cranium is part of an animal's **skeleton**. It is the bowl-shaped **bone** which grows around the brain in **vertebrate** animals. The cranium protects the **brain** from damage.

Crassigyrinus *noun*
Crassigyrinus was an **amphibian** which lived in the **Carboniferous Period**. It had a fish-like body, with a long, flexible tail. Unlike fish, it also had four tiny limbs on its body. These may have helped *Crassigyrinus* to clamber about. *Crassigyrinus* had a heavy head and a large mouth with sharp teeth. It may have lunged at its prey of fish in shallow ponds. The fish would have been sucked in as *Crassigyrinus* opened its huge mouth.

crawling ammonite ► ammonite

creeping horsetail ► horsetail

creodont *noun*
A creodont was one of a group of **mammals**. The creodonts include the ancestors of today's **carnivores**. They lived in the **Paleocene** and **Eocene Epochs**. Most creodonts were cat-like animals with short legs and a long tail. Some were larger, and included species with long, sabre-like teeth.

Cretaceous Period ► page 38

crinoid *noun*
A crinoid is a kind of **echinoderm**. The crinoids are also known as sea lilies or feather stars. There are about 625 species of crinoid known today. They are most common in the tropical parts of the Pacific Ocean. Crinoids have long, branching, feathery arms which they use to filter small particles of food from the sea water. Crinoids were very common in the **Paleozoic Era**. Some kinds of **limestone** are formed from the remains of huge numbers of crinoid skeletons. More rarely, whole crinoids are preserved as **fossils**.

crocodile ► crocodilian

crocodilian *noun*
A crocodilian is a **reptile**. The 22 species of living crocodilian are the crocodiles, alligators and the gavial. The crocodilians first appeared in the **Triassic Period** and were numerous in the **Jurassic Period**.

Cro-Magnon people *noun*
Cro-Magnon people were an early type of
human. They lived in Europe around 30,000
to 40,000 years ago. Cro-Magnon people
used tools and fire and probably wore simple
clothing. They made some cave paintings
which help us to understand how they lived.

crustacean *noun*
A crustacean is a kind of **arthropod**. There
are about 39,000 living species of
crustacean. They include crabs, lobsters,
shrimps, woodlice and water fleas.
Crustaceans first appeared in the **Cambrian
Period**.

Cryptocleidus *noun*
Cryptocleidus was a marine **reptile** which
lived in the **Jurassic Period**. It belonged to
a group called the **plesiosaurs**.
Cryptocleidus was about three metres in
length, with a long neck and tail, and four
paddle-like feet. It swam swiftly in search of
fish in the sea.

cycad *noun*
A cycad is a kind of **plant**. Cycads are
gymnosperms belonging to the order
Cycadales. There are about 70 different
species of cycad, found in tropical and sub-
tropical Central America, southern Africa,
eastern Asia and Australia. Cycads look like
palms, with a single, thick trunk and a circle
of feathery leaves. They can grow to about
15 metres. Fossil cycads have been found
from the **Jurassic** and **Cretaceous Periods**.

cycadeoid ► **bennettite**

Cynodictis *noun*
Cynodictis was a kind of dog. It lived in the
Eocene Epoch, in Europe. *Cynodictis* had a
long body and short legs.

cynodont *noun*
A cynodont was a mammal-like **reptile**.
Cynodonts first appeared in the late
Permian Period. They were **carnivorous**
and rather like dogs in shape. The ancestors
of **mammals** belonged to this group of
reptiles.

Cynognathus *noun*
Cynognathus was a mammal-like **reptile**,
belonging to the **cynodont** group. It lived in
the **Triassic Period**, and its remains have
been found in South America. Unlike other
reptiles, the body of *Cynognathus* had hair
and whiskers, like a mammal. *Cynognathus*
had a body like a dog, with a short tail. It
grew to about two metres long and fed on
smaller animals.

Cretaceous Period *noun*

The Cretaceous Period was a time in **geological history**. The Cretaceous Period lasted from about 144 million years ago to about 65 million years ago. Many huge **dinosaurs** and **flying reptiles** lived in the Cretaceous Period. Placental **mammals** first appeared at this time. At the end of the Cretaceous Period, the dinosaurs became extinct. Scientists are not sure why this happened. Mammals and plants started to evolve into many different forms.

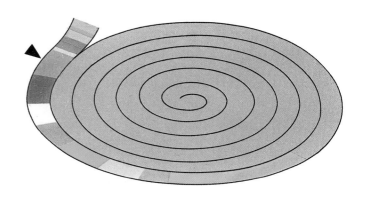

The arrow shows where the Cretaceous Period lies in relation to the geological history of the Earth.

1. *Quetzalcoatlus*
2. *Zalambdalestes*
3. *Mosasaurus*
4. *Hadrosaurus*
5. *Hesperornis*
6. *Iguanodon*
7. *Pteranodon*
8. *Pentaceratops*
9. *Elasmosaurus*
10. *Hypsilophodon*
11. *Archelon*
12. *Tyrannosaurus*

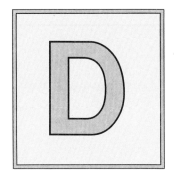

dawn redwood ▶ **Metasequoia**

decay   *verb*
Decay describes the gradual changes that take place in **radioactive** substances. Radioactive elements give off radioactive particles as they decay. **Rocks** and **fossils** can be dated by measuring the amount of **radiation** present. Decay also means **decompose** or rot.

decomposition   *noun*
Decomposition is the breaking down of a chemical substance into simpler substances. During the decomposition of animals and plants, complicated organic molecules are broken down into simpler molecules in the ground. Decomposition stops when an organism is **fossilized**.
decompose   *verb*

Deinonychus   *noun*
Deinonychus was a **carnivorous dinosaur** which lived in the **Cretaceous Period**. *Deinonychus* was about three metres long and had powerful hind legs, with large, sharp claws. The smaller front feet also had claws. Its massive jaws had sharp, pointed teeth.

Deinotherium   *noun*
Deinotherium was a kind of elephant. It lived from the **Miocene** until the **Pleistocene Epochs**, in Asia, Europe and Africa. Like today's elephants, *Deinotherium* had a long, flexible trunk. It also had tusks, but these came from the lower jaw and pointed downwards. *Deinotherium* stood about four metres tall at the shoulder.

deposit   *noun*
A deposit is any material laid down by another. The water in a river leaves a deposit of gravel and mud on its bed. Hard water leaves a deposit of calcium carbonate. When animal or plant remains become trapped in a deposit, they may turn into **fossils**.

Devonian Period ▶ page 41

Diadectes   *noun*
Diadectes was an **amphibian** which lived in the **Permian Period**. It was a reptile-like animal, coming somewhere between the **amphibians** and true **reptiles**. *Diadectes* was one of the earliest known four-legged **herbivores**.

Diademodon   *noun*
Diademodon was a mammal-like **reptile**. It lived in southern Africa during the **Triassic Period**. *Diademodon* had short legs and grew to about 1.5 metres long. It probably looked like a large rat, and fed mainly on plants.

diapsid   *noun*
The diapsids are one of the main groups of **reptiles**. They include all living reptiles except the turtles. The diapsids first appeared during the **Carboniferous Period**. Most extinct reptiles, including the **dinosaurs**, also belonged to this group. The other groups are the **anapsids** and the **synapsids**.

Devonian Period *noun*

The Devonian Period was a time in **geological history**. The Devonian Period lasted from about 410 million years ago to about 360 million years ago. **Amphibians** first came onto the land during the Devonian Period. Horsetails and club mosses grew on the land, and **insects** appeared. These early insects had no wings.

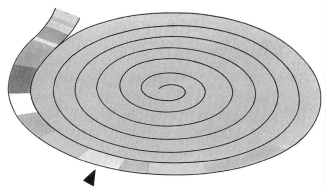

The arrow shows where the Devonian Period lies in relation to the geological history of the Earth.

1. *Icthyostega*
2. *Dunkleosteus*
3. eurypterid
4. osteichthian fish

dinosaur   *noun*

A dinosaur was a kind of **reptile** that lived between 220 million years ago and 63 million years ago. All dinosaurs are now extinct. There are two main groups of dinosaurs. The saurischian, or lizard-hipped group and the ornithischian, or bird-hipped group. The saurischians include the carnivorous theropods and the heavy, long-necked sauropods, which were plant eaters. The ornithischians were all herbivorous. They include ankylosaurs, ceratopsians and ornithopods.

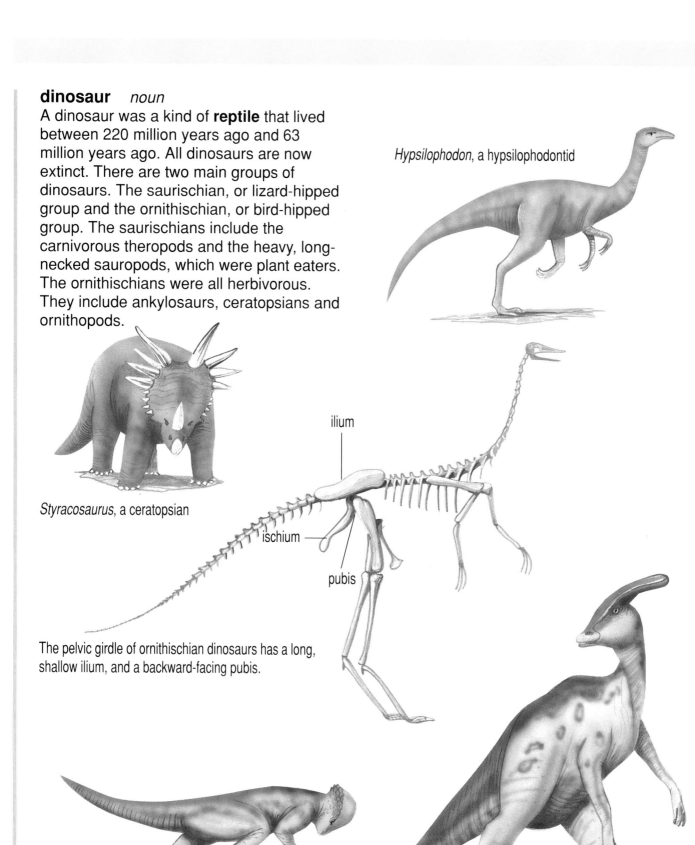

Hypsilophodon, a hypsilophodontid

ilium

ischium

pubis

Styracosaurus, a ceratopsian

The pelvic girdle of ornithischian dinosaurs has a long, shallow ilium, and a backward-facing pubis.

Stegoceras, a pachycephalosaur

Parasaurolophus, a hadrosaur

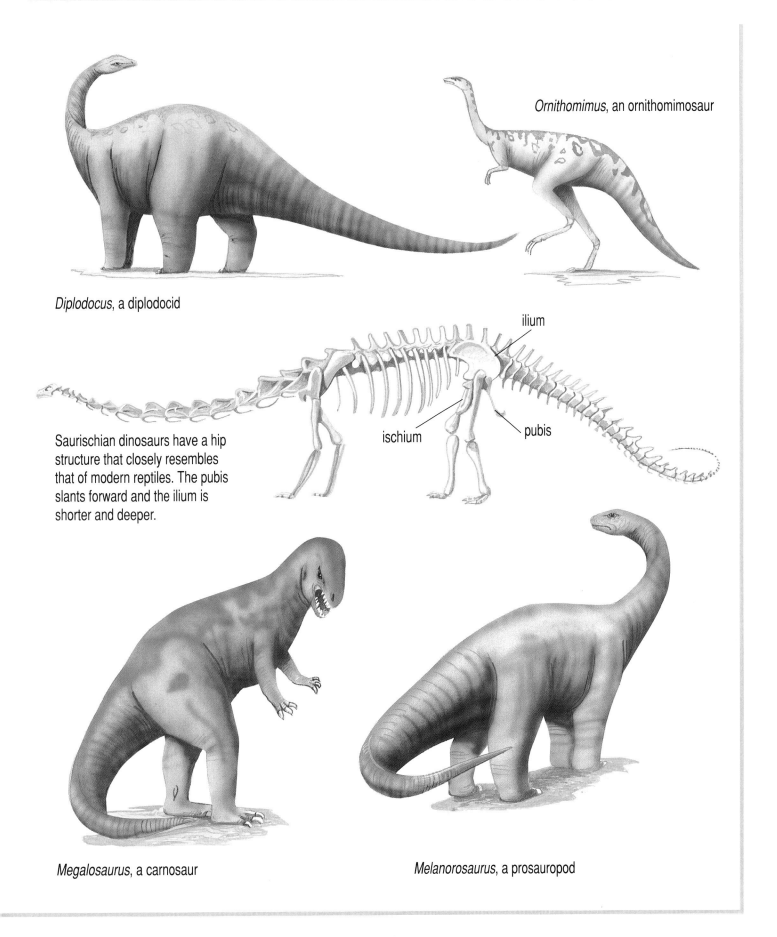

Ornithomimus, an ornithomimosaur

Diplodocus, a diplodocid

ilium

Saurischian dinosaurs have a hip structure that closely resembles that of modern reptiles. The pubis slants forward and the ilium is shorter and deeper.

ischium

pubis

Megalosaurus, a carnosaur

Melanorosaurus, a prosauropod

Diatryma *noun*
Diatryma was a large **bird**. It lived in the **Eocene Epoch**, in Europe and North America. *Diatryma* was flightless and had powerful claws and a large beak. It grew to a height of about two metres. *Diatryma* was a fierce predator, probably feeding on small mammals.

Dicerorhinus *noun*
Dicerorhinus was a kind of **rhinoceros**. It lived in the **Pliocene Epoch**. *Dicerorhinus* looked very similar to living rhinoceroses, but was smaller and had longer legs.

Dicksonia *noun*
Dicksonia is a **genus** of **tree fern**. There are about 25 species, still found in the tropics. Some grow to about 15 metres in height. Tree ferns like *Dicksonia* first appeared in the **Permian Period**.

Dicynodon *noun*
Dicynodon was a mammal-like **reptile** from southern Africa. It lived in the **Permian** and **Triassic Periods**. *Dicynodon* had few teeth, but cut up its plant food with its horny jaws.

Didymograptus *noun*
Didymograptus was an **invertebrate** which belonged to the **graptolite** group. It was about 10 centimetres long and lived floating in the sea, during the **Ordovician Period**. Groups of *Didymograptus* **fossils** formed colonies shaped like tuning forks.

Dilophosaurus *noun*
Dilophosaurus was a **dinosaur** which lived in the **Jurassic Period**. It belonged to the **carnosaur** group. *Dilophosaurus* was about six metres long. Its jaws were equipped with long, sharp teeth and it had two crests on its head. *Dilophosaurus* may have been a scavenger rather than killing for itself.

Dimetrodon *noun*
Dimetrodon was a **reptile** which lived in the **Permian Period**, in North America. It was a member of the **synapsid** group. *Dimetrodon* is known as the sail-backed lizard because of the large **sail** on its back. The sail was formed from skin stretched between long spines. *Dimetrodon* grew to about three metres long. It had sharp teeth.

Dimorphodon *noun*
Dimorphodon was a flying reptile, or **pterosaur**. Its fossils have been found in southern England. *Dimorphodon* lived in the **Jurassic Period**. It was about one metre long and had a large head and wings like those of a bat. *Dimorphodon* probably flew over the coast, feeding on fish.

Dinichthys *noun*
Dinichthys was a kind of **fish**. It was an early type of jawed fish, belonging to the group known as the **placoderms**. *Dinichthys* lived during the **Devonian Period**. It had thick, armoured skin and grew to about nine metres long. It had a tapering body, and its large mouth contained sharp teeth.

Dinilysia   *noun*
Dinilysia was a **snake** which lived in the
Cretaceous Period, in South America. It is
one of the earliest snakes known. It grew to
about three metres long, and probably fed
on small vertebrates. *Dinilysia* was not
poisonous, but killed its prey by squeezing it.

Dinoceras   *noun*
Dinoceras was a **mammal** from the **Eocene
Epoch**. It was rather like a rhinoceros in
shape, and stood about 1.5 metres tall.
Dinoceras had a pair of sharp, downward-
pointing teeth. It also had three pairs of bony
horns on its head.

Dinornis   *noun*
Dinornis was a large, flightless **bird** like an
emu. It is also known as a moa. Moas lived
in New Zealand but became extinct during
the last few centuries. They grew to a height
of up to three metres.

dinosaur ► page 42

Diplocaulus   *noun*
Diplocaulus was an early **amphibian**. It lived
in the **Permian Period**, and its **fossils** have
been found in North America and Africa.
Diplocaulus grew to about one metre long
and had a curious triangular head.

Diplodocus   *noun*
Diplodocus was a **herbivorous dinosaur**
which lived in the **Jurassic Period**. It
belonged to the **sauropod** group.
Diplodocus was up to 27 metres long. It lived
on land.

Diprotodon   *noun*
Diprotodon was a **marsupial mammal** from
the **Pleistocene Epoch**. It lived in Australia.
Diprotodon is also known as the giant
wombat. It had a body like a wombat, but
was the size of a rhinoceros, growing to
about three metres long. *Diprotodon* lived in
the forests and fed on leaves and other plant
food.

Doedicurus   *noun*
Doedicurus was a large **mammal** which
lived in South America during the
Pleistocene Epoch. It was like a giant
armadillo, and had a long tail with a heavy,
mace-like tip.

dolmen   *noun*
A dolmen was a structure built by **neolithic**
people in parts of western Europe. It was
made up of a chamber of stone blocks, with
a doorway made of larger stones. Dolmens
were probably used by these early people as
burial chambers.

dragonfly   *noun*
A dragonfly is an **insect**. It has a long, thin
body and four large wings. Dragonflies
belong to the order *Odonata*. There are
about 5,000 species of dragonfly alive today.
They feed on smaller insects. Dragonflies
first appeared in the **Carboniferous Period**.
Some extinct dragonflies were very large,
with a wingspan of more than 70
centimetres.

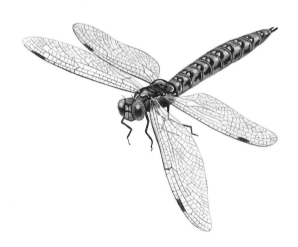

dromaeosaur   *noun*

A dromaeosaur was one of a group of **dinosaurs**. The dromaeosaurs belonged to the **theropod** group and lived during the **Cretaceous Period**. The dromaeosaurs had quite large brains.

Dromaeosaurus   *noun*

Dromaeosaurus was a small **dinosaur** which lived in the **Cretaceous Period**. Its fossils have been found in Canada. *Dromaeosaurus* had sharp claws on its feet, like *Deinonychus*. It grew to a length of about two metres.

Dryopithecus   *noun*

Dryopithecus was an early, human-like ape, or **hominoid**. It lived in the **Miocene Epoch**, about 17 million years ago. The remains of *Dryopithecus* have been found in southern Europe. It probably lived in the forests and climbed trees.

Dryosaurus   *noun*

Dryosaurus was a **dinosaur** which lived in the **Jurassic Period**. It belonged to the **ornithopod** group. Fossils of *Dryosaurus* have been found in Africa and North America. *Dryosaurus* grew to a length of about 3.5 metres and could probably run very quickly on its long, powerful hind legs. This helped it to escape from predators. *Dryosaurus* fed on plants.

duck-billed dinosaur ▶ **hadrosaur**

Dunkleosteus   *noun*

Dunkleosteus was a **fish** which lived in the **Devonian Period**. It belonged to the group known as the **placoderms**. Most placoderms were small, but *Dunkleosteus* reached a length of 10 metres.

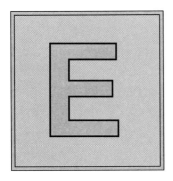

echinoderm *noun*
An echinoderm is an **invertebrate** animal. The echinoderm **phylum** includes starfish, sea urchins, sea cucumbers and **crinoids**. The earliest echinoderms were the crinoids and **echinoids**. These appeared as early as the **Cambrian Period**. All echinoderms live in the sea, and many have spiny skin.

echinoid *noun*
An echinoid is an **invertebrate** animal. Echinoids form part of the **echinoderm** phylum. They are the sea urchins and their relatives. The skeletons of echinoids are often found as **fossils**. The earliest known echinoids are from the **Ordovician Period**. They were common in the **Mesozoic Era**.

Edaphosaurus *noun*
Edaphosaurus was a **synapsid reptile**. It lived in the **Carboniferous** and **Permian Periods**, in Europe and North America. *Edaphosaurus* was about three metres long and had a tall **sail** on its back. It is also called the sail-backed lizard. *Edaphosaurus* lived in hot, dry areas and probably used its sail to control its body temperature. In the morning, it would stand sideways on to the Sun. The Sun then warmed the blood flowing through the sail.

Ediacaran fauna *noun*
The Ediacaran fauna was a group of animals. They were the earliest known many-celled animals. The Ediacaran fauna lived about 630 million years ago, in the **Precambrian Period**. These animals were all **invertebrates**, with a soft body.

Edmontosaurus *noun*
Edmontosaurus, or the duck-billed dinosaur, lived in the **Cretaceous Period**. It belonged to the **ornithopod** group. It was about 13 metres long and its most noticeable feature was its broad, duck-like snout. *Edmontosaurus* may have been partly aquatic, and fed on plants. **Fossils** of *Edmontosaurus* have been found in North America.

Elasmosaurus *noun*
Elasmosaurus was a dinosaur which lived in the **Cretaceous Period**. It belonged to the **plesiosaur** group. It grew to a length of about 15 metres, of which more than half was taken up with its long, thin neck. Most **vertebrates** have only seven neck vertebrae, but *Elasmosaurus* and its relatives had up to seventy-five. Like all plesiosaurs, *Elasmosaurus* lived in water. It swam well using its four paddle-like feet. *Elasmosaurus* hunted fish, catching them with its sharp teeth.

Elasmotherium *noun*
Elasmotherium was a **mammal** which lived in the **Pleistocene Epoch**. It was a large **ungulate** similar to a rhinoceros, and is sometimes known as the woolly rhinoceros. It had a huge horn on its nose and a very heavy body. It also had thick fur to keep out the cold. *Elasmotherium* lived in Asia and Europe. It fed on the grasses, lichens and low bushes of the tundra.

Eocene Epoch   *noun*

The Eocene Epoch was a time in **geological history**. The Eocene Epoch lasted from about 55 million years ago to about 38 million years ago. The first **ungulates** appeared during the Eocene Epoch. Many ancestors of modern mammals also evolved. Fossil frogs dating from the Eocene Epoch are not very different from modern frogs.

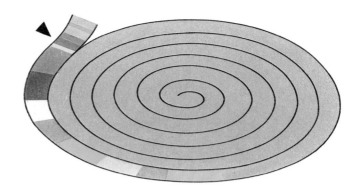

The arrow shows where the Eocene Epoch lies in relation
to the geological history of the Earth.

1. *Icaronycteris*
2. *Uintatherium*
3. *Notharctus*
4. *Eomanis*
5. *Archaeotherium*
6. *Diatryma*
7. *Moeritherium*
8. *Hyracotherium*

embryo *noun*
An embryo is a stage in the growth of an animal. It is the earliest stage after fertilization has taken place. In most **mammals**, the embryo forms inside the mother's body. In animals which lay eggs, the embryo grows inside the egg yolk until it hatches.

Eocene Epoch ▶ page 48

Eogyrinus *noun*
Eogyrinus was an early form of **amphibian**. It lived in the water, like some salamanders and newts. However, it was very large, up to 4.5 metres long, and had fearsome jaws with sharp teeth. *Eogyrinus* probably ate fish and other amphibians.

Eohippus ▶ **Hyracotherium**

Eomanis *noun*
Eomanis was a small scaly anteater, or pangolin, from the **Eocene Epoch**. Its fossil was discovered in Germany in 1978. *Eomanis* is the oldest known pangolin. Like living pangolins, *Eomanis* was covered in scales and could curl up when frightened. It fed on ants.

eon *noun*
An eon is one of the divisions of **geological history**. There are four eons, the **Azoic**, the **Archean**, the **Proterozoic** and the **Phanerozoic**. Each eon is divided into **eras** and **periods**. All the periods from the **Cambrian** to the present day are part of the Phanerozoic Eon.

Ephedra *noun*
Ephedra is an unusual kind of **gymnosperm** plant. There are about 40 species known, mostly from North America, South America, the Mediterranean region and Asia. *Ephedra* has thin, green, strap-like leaves and small flowers. Related plants are known from the **Cretaceous Period**.

Epigaulus *noun*
Epigaulus was a small **mammal** from the **Miocene Epoch**. It was a burrowing **rodent** from North America. *Epigaulus* looked rather like a dumpy prairie dog. Its strangest feature was the pair of horns at the end of its nose.

epoch *noun*
An epoch is a division of **geological history**. Each **period** of the **Cenozoic Era** is divided into epochs. The epoch today is called the **Holocene** or **Recent Epoch**.

Equus *noun*
Equus is the horse. It evolved in the **Pleistocene Epoch** and still survives. Today, wild horses are almost extinct, and most horses are domesticated forms. Wild horses often feature in **cave art**.

era *noun*
An era is one of the main divisions of **geological history**. Each era is divided into **periods**. The order of eras from oldest to youngest is Paleozoic, Mesozoic and Cenozoic.

erosion *noun*
Erosion is the wearing down of rocks or soils. It is caused by the action of water, wind or ice, or by living **organisms**. Erosion may remove fertile soil from farmland and hillsides.

Eryops *noun*
Eryops was an **amphibian** which lived in the **Carboniferous** and **Permian Periods**. It had longer legs than other early amphibians and spent much of its life on land. Frogs and toads probably evolved from animals such as *Eryops*.

Erythrosuchus *noun*
Erythrosuchus was a carnivorous **reptile** which lived in the **Triassic Period**. It belonged to the **thecodont** group. *Erythrosuchus* was about 4.5 metres long and looked rather like a crocodile.

Estemmenosuchus *noun*
Estemmenosuchus was a mammal-like **reptile**. It lived in the **Permian Period** and its fossils have been found in Russia. *Estemmenosuchus* was about four metres long and had a stout body with short horns on its head. It was probably mainly **herbivorous**.

Euoplocephalus *noun*
Euoplocephalus was a **dinosaur** which lived in the **Cretaceous Period**. It belonged to the **ornithischian** group. *Euoplocephalus* is known as the armoured dinosaur, and had hard, bony plates and spikes along its back. Its tail ended in a heavy, bony club.

Euparkeria *noun*
Euparkeria was a small, carnivorous **reptile** from the **Triassic Period**. It belonged to the **thecodont** group, and its fossils come from South Africa. *Euparkeria* was only about the size of a large hen. It ran about on its long back legs, but also walked on all fours.

euryapsids *noun*
The euryapsids were a group of **reptiles**. They include the **plesiosaurs**, the **notosaurs** and the **placodonts**. They lived from the **Permian Period** until the late **Cretaceous Period**. The other reptile groups are the **anapsids**, the **diapsids** and the **synapsids**.

eurypterid *noun*
A eurypterid, or water scorpion, was an **arthropod**. It lived from the **Ordovician Period** until the **Permian Period**. Eurypterids were related to king crabs, and had a hard **carapace** and paddle-like limbs. Some reached a length of nearly two metres. Most eurypterids lived in the sea, but some went into fresh water, and a few may have gone onto land.

evolution ▶ page 52

excavate *verb*
Excavate describes the process of digging carefully into the ground. **Geologists** and **paleontologists** excavate quarries and cliffs when looking for fossils or rock formations.
excavation *noun*

extinct *adjective*
Extinct describes a species of animal or plant which has disappeared completely from the Earth. When it is extinct, it cannot be replaced in its original form. The **dinosaurs** were once common, but are now extinct.

evolution *noun*

Evolution describes the gradual changes that take place in the bodies of animals and plants. The changes may happen over thousands or millions of years. Scientists believe that the changes occur as the animal or plant slowly adapts to a changing environment. Not all the adaptations are successful, and some species become **extinct**. An evolving species may develop a new characteristic. It may become bigger, or the shape of its body may change.

evolve *verb*

Equus, or the modern horse, has a wide range of vision and can run fast. Most of the different breeds seen today have not evolved naturally. They have come about by selective breeding.

Evolution of the horse

Hyracotherium, also called *Eohippus* or dawn horse, lived in the Eocene Epoch. It was only about 30 centimetres tall. It had four toes on its front feet and three toes at the back.

Przewalski's horse is the only true wild horse that exists today. It is a different species from the domestic horse.

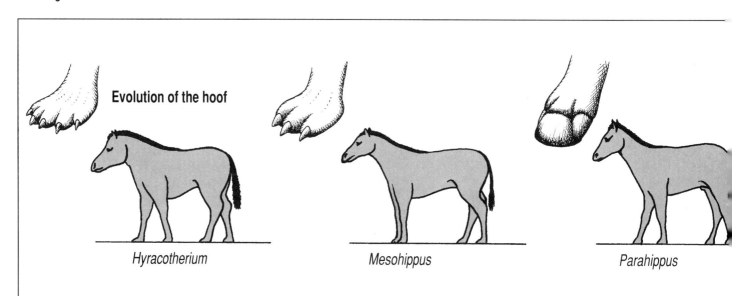

Evolution of the hoof

Hyracotherium

Mesohippus

Parahippus

Mesohippus lived in the Oligocene Epoch. It had three toes on its feet, and measured about 60 centimetres. It probably hid from its enemies instead of running away.

Parahippus first appeared in the Miocene Epoch. By this time the climate was becoming drier. The swamps were gradually changing into prairies.

Pliohippus was 1.25 metres tall. It had strong limbs and was a fast runner.

Hipparion lived on open grasslands in the Pliocene Epoch.

Hipparion

Equus

fish *noun*

A fish is a **vertebrate** that lives in water. Fish breathe under water through their gills. The body of most fish is covered with scales. Many fish have skeletons made of bone, but fish such as sharks have skeletons made of cartilage. The first fish appeared in the **Ordovician Period**. They were jawless fish, or **agnathans**, and many of them had hard, scaly armour-plating for protection. Later fish developed jaws which made it easier for them to catch their prey.

Development of a jaw

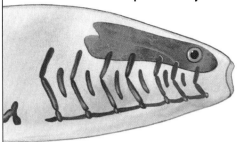

Pharyngolepis had several pairs of gills strengthened by an arch of bone. Jawless fish either sieved food out of the water or rasped at lumps of food with horny teeth.

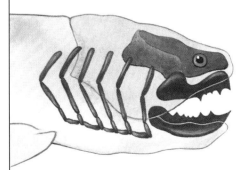

Coccosteus had fewer gill slits. The arch of bone as found in *Pharyngolepis* had developed to form two hinged jaws. Jaws allowed fish to bite and chew on large lumps of food.

Pteraspis was an early jawless fish. It was about 25 centimetres long. It had no paired fins, and swam by wriggling, like a tadpole.

Bothriolepis had armour-plating on the front of its body, and lived in fresh water.

54

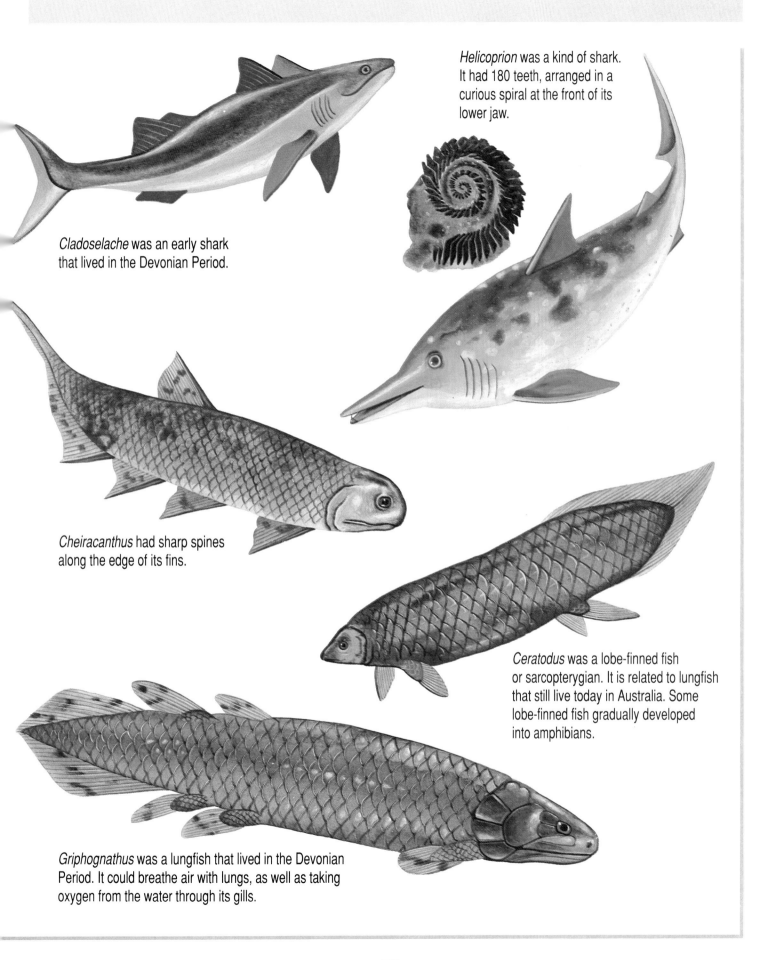

Helicoprion was a kind of shark. It had 180 teeth, arranged in a curious spiral at the front of its lower jaw.

Cladoselache was an early shark that lived in the Devonian Period.

Cheiracanthus had sharp spines along the edge of its fins.

Ceratodus was a lobe-finned fish or sarcopterygian. It is related to lungfish that still live today in Australia. Some lobe-finned fish gradually developed into amphibians.

Griphognathus was a lungfish that lived in the Devonian Period. It could breathe air with lungs, as well as taking oxygen from the water through its gills.

Fabrosaurus *noun*
Fabrosaurus was a small **dinosaur** from the **Jurassic Period**. It was one of the first of the bird-footed dinosaurs, or **ornithopods**. *Fabrosaurus* was about one metre long. It had a sturdy tail and long back legs. Its fossils have been found in southern Africa. *Fabrosaurus* was a plant-eater, or **herbivore**.

family *noun*
A family is part of the classification system of living things. All animals and plants belonging to the same family share certain features, or characteristics. Each family contains one or more **genera**. The family lies between **order** and **genus** in the classification system.

fauna *noun*
Fauna is the animal life of a region or habitat. It includes the tiny animals of the soil and water as well as more obvious, larger animals such as **mammals** and **birds**. The **dinosaurs** were the most widespread and strongest land fauna found in the **Jurassic Period**.

fern *noun*
A fern is a kind of **plant**. Ferns form part of the division *Pteridophyta*. They are feathery, green plants which mostly grow in wet or damp places. There are over 10,000 species of fern found all over the world. The damp, tropical regions have the greatest number of ferns. Scientists think that ferns first appeared on Earth more than 350 million years ago, during the **Devonian Period**.

fin *noun*
A fin is a flap sticking out from the body of an animal. Fish have fins, and so do marine mammals such as whales and dolphins. Extinct **aquatic reptiles** such as the **plesiosaurs** also had fins. Fins are used by an aquatic animal for swimming and for keeping it steady in the water.

fir *noun*
A fir is a kind of **coniferous tree**. Firs belong to the genus *Abies*. There are around 40 species of fir, in Europe, Asia, North America and Central America. The giant fir of north-west America grows to 100 metres high. **Fossils** of fir trees have been found dating from the **Cretaceous Period**.

fish ► page 54

flint *noun*
Flint is a kind of **rock**. Flints are usually found as grey or brown pebbles in chalk. They come in many shapes and sizes. **Fossils** are often preserved in flint nodules. Early people made sharp tools by breaking and sharpening flint.

flora *noun*
Flora is the plant life of a region or habitat. It includes the tiny mosses and liverworts, as well as large plants such as shrubs and trees. The flora of an area depends on its soil and climate, and on its history. People have altered the natural flora over much of the world.

flowering plant ► **angiosperm**

flying reptile ► page 58

foliage *noun*
Foliage is the word used for the leaves and shoots of green **plants**. Many animals, including large numbers of dinosaurs, feed or fed on foliage. Animals which eat foliage usually have sharp teeth or jaws to bite it off, and flat teeth to grind it up.

food chain   *noun*
A food chain is the pattern of food energy which is passed from one living thing to another. **Plants** are at the bottom of food chains. Plants are eaten by **herbivores**, which in turn provide food for **carnivores**. These carnivores may then be eaten by other carnivores at the top of food chains.

footprint   *noun*
A footprint is the mark left behind by an animal's foot. Footprints can often be found in sand or soft mud. Sometimes, the footprints left behind by extinct animals became preserved as **trace fossils**. These fossil footprints tell scientists something about how **dinosaurs** moved.

foraminiferan   *noun*
Foraminiferans are an **order** of tiny, one-celled animals. They belong to the kingdom *Protista*. Foraminiferans are mostly marine. Some float at the sea's surface and others live on the sea-bed. They have tiny shells. When foraminiferans die, their shells gather on the sea-bed. Here, they may fossilize to form **limestone** rock.

forelimb   *noun*
A forelimb is one of the two front legs of a four-legged animal. Many animals use their forelimbs as legs for running. In **bipeds**, the forelimbs are smaller and used as arms. In the **pterosaurs**, **birds** and **bats**, the forelimbs are wings, used for flight.

fossil   *noun*
A fossil is an **organism**, or sign of an organism, which has been preserved in **rocks**. People know about **extinct** animals and plants because scientists have studied their fossils. A fossil may be of a **footprint**, or a preserved **bone** or whole **skeleton**.

fossilization   ► page 60

frog   *noun*
A frog is an **amphibian**. There are about 3,500 species of frog and toad alive today. Most frogs live in wet habitats and return to the water to lay their eggs. Fossil frogs found in the **Eocene Epoch** differ little from those of today.

fungus (plural **fungi**)   *noun*
A fungus is a plant-like **organism**. Fungi are not plants, but belong to their own kingdom. There are over 50,000 species of fungus known, but there may be more than 100,000 species in the world. Familiar fungi include mushrooms and toadstools. Many fungi are microscopic and difficult to see. Many also live underground where they grow as long fibres. Unlike green plants, fungi have no chlorophyll and cannot make their own food. Fungi do not fossilize well, so it is hard to tell how old they are. It is known that they date back to the **Silurian Period**, and possibly to the **Precambrian Period**.

flying reptile   *noun*

A flying reptile is a **reptile** that can fly. The earliest flying animals were the **insects** that appeared in the **Carboniferous Period**. The first flying reptiles appeared in the **Permian Period**. They could not fly by flapping their wings. They were gliders. Their wings consisted of flaps of skin attached to their body. The **pterosaurs** were the first reptiles that could flap their wings. Pterosaur arm bones were long and thin. The fourth finger was elongated, and supported the wing.

Pterodactylus had claws and a beak with teeth. It probably had a furry body.

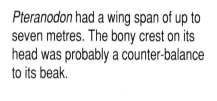

Pteranodon had a wing span of up to seven metres. The bony crest on its head was probably a counter-balance to its beak.

Kuehnosaurus had remarkably long ribs. It could spread out these ribs and glide on the skin stretched out between them.

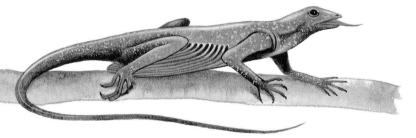

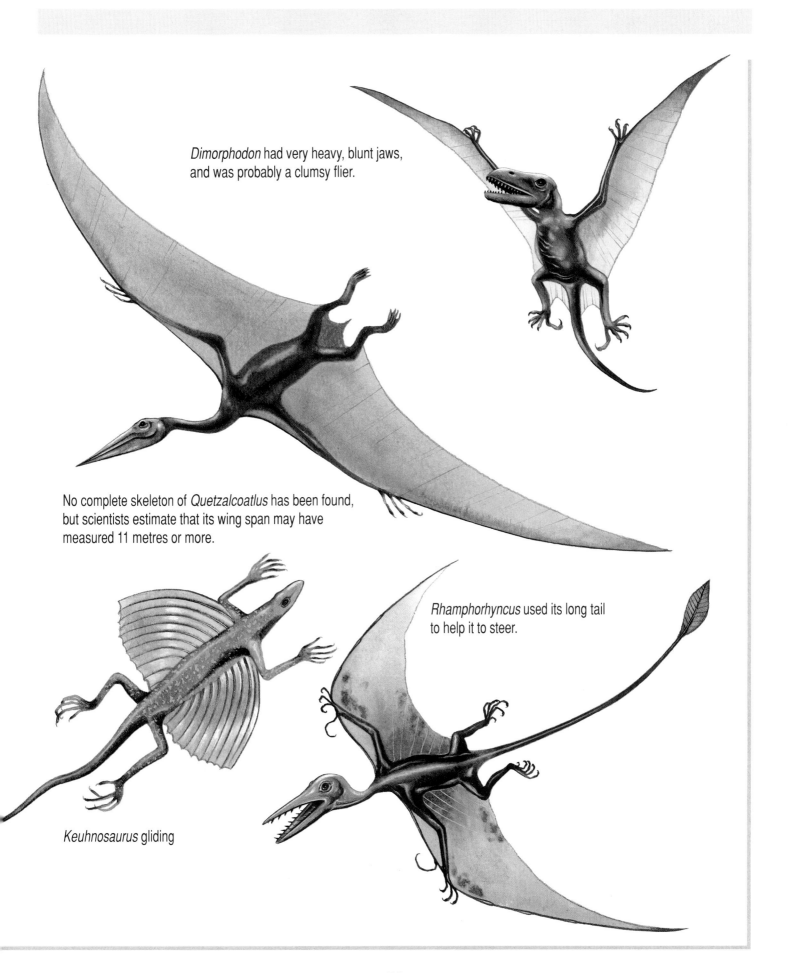

Dimorphodon had very heavy, blunt jaws, and was probably a clumsy flier.

No complete skeleton of Quetzalcoatlus has been found, but scientists estimate that its wing span may have measured 11 metres or more.

Rhamphorhyncus used its long tail to help it to steer.

Keuhnosaurus gliding

fossilization *noun*

Fossilization is the way in which remains of ancient living things are preserved. The most common fossils are the hard parts of animals and plants that have turned into **rock**. Fossilization also occurs when a living thing completely dissolves, leaving only its shape pressed into soft mud or sand. The shape becomes a kind of mould or **cast** that can be filled to show what the animal looked like.

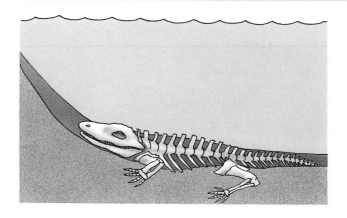

Gradually, layers of sand or mud covered the skeleton.

Millions of years ago, *Eryops* died, and its body sank to the bottom of the sea.

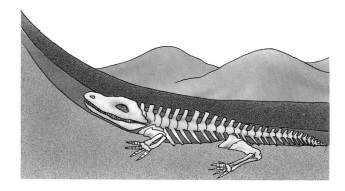

Very slowly, the bones were filled by other minerals, making them into fossils.

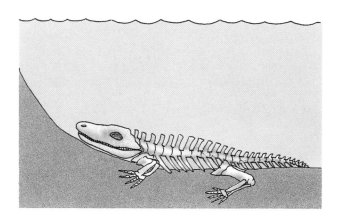

The flesh decayed or was eaten by other animals, until only the skeleton was left.

Millions of years later, the sea changed position. The layers of rock on top of the fossil were gradually worn away by wind and rain.

60

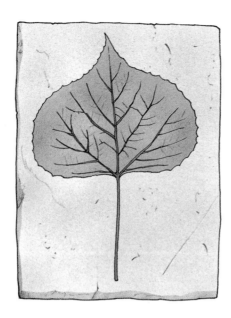

This fossilized poplar leaf is about 25 million years old. The leaf is almost exactly the same as a modern poplar leaf.

The external skeleton of this trilobite contained a hard mineral called calcite that does not decay easily. Parts of animals containing calcite are often found as fossils.

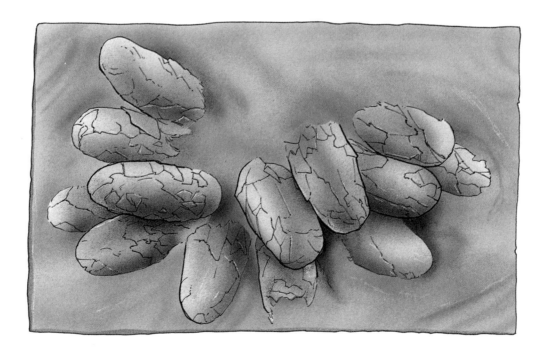

This is a cast made of a nest of *Protoceratops* eggs. The nest must have been covered in soft sand and mud shortly after the eggs were laid.

Gallimimus   *noun*

Gallimimus was a bird-like **dinosaur** which lived in the **Cretaceous Period**, in Asia. It had powerful legs, but its forelimbs were small. *Gallimimus* grew to a length of about six metres. It had a large, horny beak.

gastropod   *noun*

A gastropod is a **mollusc**. The gastropods make up the largest **class** of molluscs. There are about 77,000 species of gastropod alive today. Many gastropods have hard shells which preserve well as **fossils**. The earliest known gastropods come from the **Cambrian Period**.

genus (plural **genera**)   *noun*

A genus is a rank in the classification of **organisms**. The genus lies between the **species** and the **family**. Each family contains one or more genera. Species which are similar enough to each other are grouped together in the same genus.

geological history ▶ page 64

geologist   *noun*

A geologist is someone who studies the Earth. Some geologists study the history of the Earth. Some look at its structure and the processes which have formed it. Other geologists study **fossils**.

geology   *noun*

Geology is the study of the Earth. It includes a study of the Earth's structure and the processes which form it. It also includes **paleontology**, the study of **fossils**.

Geosaurus   *noun*

Geosaurus was a **crocodilian** which lived in the **Jurassic** and **Cretaceous Periods**. It was about 2.5 metres long and had a large head with many sharp teeth.

Gerrothorax   *noun*

Gerrothorax was an **amphibian**. It lived in the **Triassic Period**, and its fossils have been found in Spitzbergen and Greenland. It was like a giant tadpole, and probably had external gills. *Gerrothorax* grew to about one metre long.

Ginkgo   *noun*

Ginkgo is a **genus** of tree from China. There is only one species of *Ginkgo*, and it belongs to its own order because it is so unusual. *Ginkgo* is a tall, deciduous tree with fan-shaped leaves. It is also called the maidenhair tree. The relatives of *Ginkgo* first appeared in the **Permian Period**.

glaciation   *noun*

Glaciation is the way in which land is shaped by ice. Glaciation is also the name for the times during geological history when ice covered the Earth. During the Pleistocene **Ice Age**, as much as one third of the Earth's surface was covered with ice. Glaciations spread very gradually over the land, so many plants and animals had time to adapt to the new conditions or migrate to a warmer climate.

glacial   *adjective*

Glyptodon *noun*

Glyptodon was a giant armadillo. It lived in South America in the **Pleistocene Epoch**. *Glyptodon* was very like living armadillos, except that it was huge, measuring nearly 3.5 metres long. It became extinct only a few thousand years ago.

Gondwanaland *noun*

Gondwanaland is the name of a large **continent**. It formed when the super-continent of **Pangaea** split about 150 million years ago, during the **Mesozoic Era**. Gondwanaland gradually split further, to create South America, Antarctica, Africa, India, Australia and New Zealand.

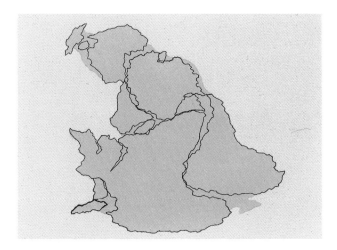

graptolite *noun*

A graptolite was an **invertebrate** animal. Graptolites lived in colonies, and were rather like leaves in shape. They lived from the **Cambrian** until the **Carboniferous Periods**. Graptolites can help **paleontologists** to date **rocks**.

grass *noun*

A grass is a **plant**. It belongs to the monocotyledon group. There are about 8,000 species of grass in the world. Grasses have long, narrow leaves and rounded, hollow stems. The flowers of grasses are rather small and dull. The fruit of a grass is a grain. Most cereal crops are grasses. Sugar cane is also a kind of grass. Many animals feed on grass.

grazer *noun*

A grazer is an animal which feeds mainly by eating **grass**. Many extinct animals were grazers. Living grazers include horses, zebras and antelopes.
graze *verb*

green alga (plural **algae**) *noun*

Green algae are a group of plants. They include the stoneworts, seaweeds and many tiny, microscopic plants. Most green algae live in fresh water or damp soil. There are about 25,000 species of green algae alive today. Green algae first appeared in the **Cambrian Period**.

ground sloth ► Megatherium

gymnosperm *noun*

A gymnosperm is a type of **plant**. The gymnosperms form the class *Gymnospermae*, which contains about 700 species. Gymnosperms include the **conifers**, and also smaller groups such as **cycads** and the *Ginkgo*. The gymnosperms include the world's largest and oldest trees. Gymnosperms formed the main vegetation during the **Jurassic** and early **Cretaceous Periods**. They first appeared during the **Carboniferous Period**. **Coal** is formed largely from the remains of fossil gymnosperms.

geological history *noun*

Geological history describes the way scientists divide up the time since the Earth has been in existence. It is thought that the Earth was formed about 4,600 million years ago. The largest divisions in geological history are the **eons**. The most recent eon is divided into three **eras**. Each era is further divided into a number of periods or epochs. The **Quaternary** sub-era began nearly two million years ago, and still continues today.

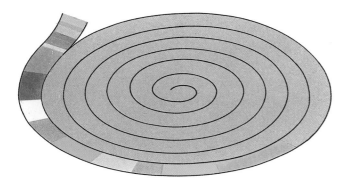

This coil shows how recently life has evolved on Earth. For most of the Earth's 4,600 million year history, there were no living things at all.

Eon	Era	Period/Epoch	
Phanerozoic	Cenozoic (Quaternary)	Pleistocene Epoch	
	Cenozoic (Tertiary)	Pliocene Epoch	
	Cenozoic (Tertiary)	Miocene Epoch	
	Cenozoic (Tertiary)	Oligocene Epoch	
	Cenozoic (Tertiary)	Eocene Epoch	
	Cenozoic (Tertiary)	Paleocene Epoch	
	Mesozoic	Cretaceous Period	
	Mesozoic	Jurassic Period	
	Mesozoic	Triassic Period	
	Paleozoic	Permian Period	
	Paleozoic	Carboniferous Period	
	Paleozoic	Devonian Period	
	Paleozoic	Silurian Period	
	Paleozoic	Ordovician Period	
	Paleozoic	Cambrian Period	
Proterozoic		Precambrian Period	
Archean			

s of years ago	Living things	
2	Sabre-toothed cat, *Homo sapiens*	
5	Hominids, cattle, sheep	
24.5	First hominids, elephants	
38	First apes, deer	
55	First dogs, cats, rabbits, elephants, horses	
65	First carnivorous mammals	
144	First flowering plants, dinosaurs	
213	Conifers, biggest dinosaurs, first birds	
248	First dinosaurs, crocodiles, tortoises	
286	First beetles, mammal-like reptiles	
360	First reptiles, dragonflies, swampy forests, tree ferns	
408	First amphibians, insects, spiders, bony fish	
438	Eurypterids, first jawed fish, first land plants	
505	Nautiloids, trilobites, corals, brachiopods, graptolites	
590	First fish, trilobites, corals	
2,500 4,000	Jellyfish and worms	

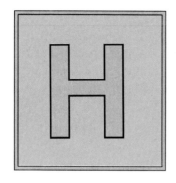

hadrosaur *noun*

A hadrosaur was one of a group of **dinosaurs** which lived in the **Cretaceous Period**. The hadrosaurs belonged to the **ornithopod** group. They were **herbivorous dinosaurs** that had up to 300 teeth in each jaw for grinding down tough vegetation. Hadrosaurs are known as duck-billed dinosaurs because of their flattened snout. Fossilized hadrosaur bones have been found in Asia and North America.

Hadrosaurus *noun*

Hadrosaurus was a large dinosaur which lived in the **Cretaceous Period**. It belonged to the **ornithopod** group. *Hadrosaurus* was about 10 metres long and stood on its hind legs. It had a flattened snout. *Hadrosaurus* was one of the duck-billed dinosaurs, or **hadrosaurs**. It was a plant-eater, or **herbivore**.

Hallucigenia *noun*

Hallucigenia was one of the first many-celled animals to live. It formed part of the famous **Burgess Shale** fauna, and lived in the **Cambrian Period**, about 570 million years ago. *Hallucigenia* was a worm-like animal supported on several pairs of stilt-like legs. It probably lived on the sea-bed.

Halysite *noun*

Halysite was a **coral**. It lived in the **Ordovician** and **Silurian Periods**. *Halysite* belonged to an extinct group of corals known as the tabulate corals.

handy people ► Homo habilis

hatchling *noun*

A hatchling is a young animal which has recently hatched from an egg. Young **birds** are usually called nestlings, but young **dinosaurs** and other **reptiles** are usually known as hatchlings. **Fossil** hatchlings have sometimes been found.

hatching hadrosaur

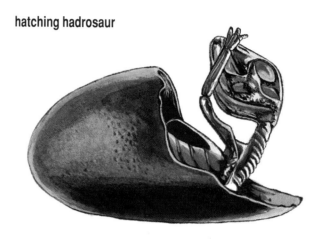

herbivore *noun*

A herbivore is an animal which eats only plant material. Herbivores have specially adapted **teeth** to grind plants, and their guts are adapted to digest plant material. Elephants and rabbits are examples of herbivores. Many extinct animals were also herbivores.

herbivorous dinosaur ► page 68

Hesperornis *noun*

Hesperornis was a **bird**. It lived in the **Cretaceous Period** and its fossilized bones have been found in North America. *Hesperornis* stood nearly two metres tall, and was flightless like a penguin. It was a swimming and diving bird which probably used its small wings as paddles under the water.

heterodontosaur *noun*

A heterodontosaur was a **dinosaur** with different kinds of teeth in its jaw. It belonged to the bird-footed group, or **ornithopods**. The heterodontosaurs are known from the upper **Triassic** to early **Jurassic Periods**.

heterotrophic *adjective*
Heterotrophic describes a kind of feeding, or nutrition. Heterotrophic organisms cannot make their own food from simple chemicals. Instead, they feed on other plants or animals. Most animals are heterotrophic. The other main kind of feeding is **autotrophic**.

hickory *noun*
Hickory is a kind of deciduous tree. It belongs to the **genus** *Carya*, and is in the same family as the walnut. Pecans, which have edible nuts, are a kind of hickory. Most kinds of hickory grow in eastern North America. In the **Pliocene Epoch**, hickory grew in Europe as well.

hindlimb *noun*
A hindlimb is one of the two back legs of a four-legged animal. In most four-legged **vertebrate** animals, the hindlimbs carry the weight of the body and are used for walking or running. Many dinosaurs only used their hind legs for moving about. They are called **bipeds**. Some mammals are also bipeds.

hip *noun*
The hip, or pelvic girdle, is part of the **skeleton** of vertebrates. It is the part where the legs join the main skeleton. There are three main bones in the hip. These are the **ilium**, the **ischium** and the **pubis**. In the two main groups of **dinosaur**, the bones of the hip are arranged differently.

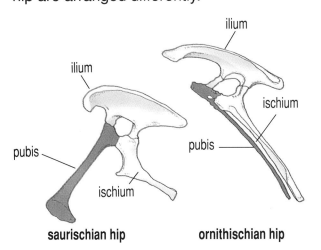

ilium

ilium

ischium

pubis

pubis

ischium

saurischian hip   **ornithischian hip**

hippopotamus *noun*
A hippopotamus is a large **mammal**. There are two species alive today, both in Africa. They have a thick body, short legs and a large head with tusk-like teeth. Hippopotamuses spend much of their time in water and graze on vegetation at the water's edge. They first appeared in the **Miocene Epoch** in Africa, about 10 million years ago.

hoatzin *noun*
The hoatzin is a **bird**. It lives along river banks and marshes in South America. Young hoatzins are born with claws on their wings. They use these to help them climb in the trees. As the young hoatzins grow, these claws drop off. Some of the ancestors of birds, such as **Archaeopteryx**, also had claws on their wings.

Holocene Epoch *noun*
The Holocene Epoch is a division in the Earth's **geological history**. It is also called the Recent Epoch, and it includes the present time. The Holocene Epoch forms part of the **Quaternary Period**. It began about 10,000 years ago.

hominid *noun*
The hominids are the **family** which includes the **human** species. Remains of the first known hominids were found in East Africa and date from the **Pliocene Epoch**, four or five million years ago. *Australopithecus* was the earliest hominid. Other hominids are *Homo habilis*, *Homo erectus* and our own species, *Homo sapiens*.

herbivorous dinosaur *noun*

A herbivorous dinosaur was a **dinosaur** that ate plants. Herbivorous dinosaurs needed to spend a lot of their time eating. Some grazed on grasses and low-growing plants. Others reached up to browse on leaves of trees. Some herbivores could move their jaws from side to side to grind the vegetation. Others had a muscular stomach in which stomach stones called gastroliths helped to break down tough fibres.

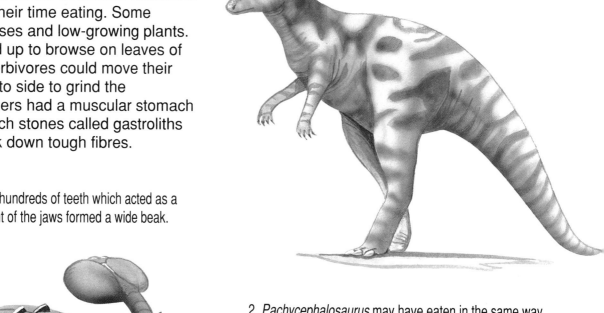

1. *Anatosaurus* had hundreds of teeth which acted as a rasping file. The front of the jaws formed a wide beak.

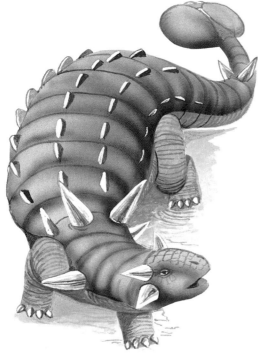

2. *Pachycephalosaurus* may have eaten in the same way as a modern sheep.

The shapes below show the size of each dinosaur compared with a man.

3. *Kentosaurus* probably used its jaws to bite off plant food. Food was swallowed quickly and left to ferment in the large stomach.

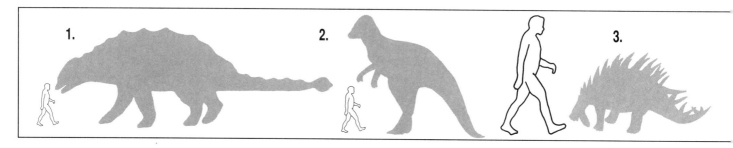

1.　　　　　2.　　　　　3.

4. *Plateosaurus* had roughly serrated teeth. It fed on plants at ground level and on tall trees. There were probably gastroliths in its stomach to help break down the food.

5. *Brachiosaurus* browsed on high-growing vegetation with its large, chisel-shaped teeth.

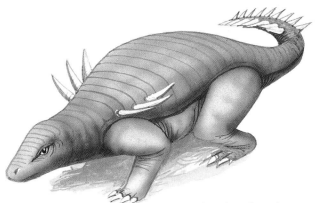

6. *Silvisaurus* had eight or nine small pointed teeth at the front of the upper jaw. Other dinosaurs in the ankylosaur group only had a horny beak.

7. *Triceratops* had rows of cheek teeth for grinding vegetation.

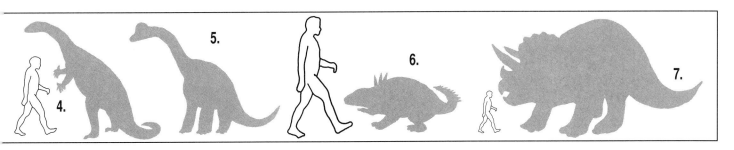

5.

6.

7.

4.

hominid evolution ► page 72

hominoid *noun*
The hominoids are a group which includes
the apes and **humans**. They share features
of body structure and body chemistry. Apes
and humans differ mainly in brain size,
posture and diet.

Homo erectus *noun*
Homo erectus was a type of **hominid**. It
lived from about 1.6 million years ago until
about 100,000 years ago. Skeletons of
Homo erectus have been found in Asia,
Europe and Africa. Like modern people,
Homo erectus had a large brain and knew
how to use tools and make fire.

Homo habilis *noun*
Homo habilis was a type of **hominid**. It lived
around 1.75 million years ago. Bones of
Homo habilis have been found in East
Africa. *Homo habilis* was smaller than **Homo
erectus**, but it had a larger skull than earlier
hominids. *Homo habilis* probably lived by
hunting in the savanna.

Homo sapiens *noun*
Homo sapiens is the scientific name for our
own species. We are the most highly
evolved of all the **hominids**. *Homo sapiens*
with a modern appearance first came onto
the scene about 100,000 years ago, in
Africa. **Neanderthal people** are regarded as
a form of *Homo sapiens*.

horn *noun*
A horn is a structure sticking out from an
animal's head. Many **dinosaurs** had horns.
Modern animals with horns include
antelopes, cows and rhinoceroses. Horns
are usually made of bone, but the rhino's
horn is made of tightly-packed hair. Deer
have horns which are shed each year. They
are known as antlers.

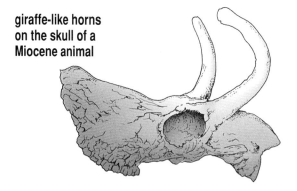

giraffe-like horns
on the skull of a
Miocene animal

horned dinosaur ► **ceratopsian**

horned head ► **ceratopsid**

horse ► **Equus**

horseshoe crab *noun*
A horseshoe crab is a marine **invertebrate**.
It is not a true crab and is more closely
related to **spiders**. There are five species of
horseshoe crab found today. They grow to
about 30 centimetres long. They have a hard
shell covering the head and a long, spiny
tail. Horseshoe crabs catch their prey using
pincers on their front pair of legs. Horseshoe
crabs similar to living species are known
from the **Jurassic** and **Cretaceous Periods**.

horsetail *noun*
A horsetail is a **plant**. Horsetails belong to
the **pteridophyte** group of plants. There are
about 30 species of horsetail. They have
jointed and ridged stems, with feathery
branches and small leaves. Horsetails
appeared in the **Devonian Period**. The most
common fossil horsetail is *Calamites*, which
grew to about 18 metres high.

human *noun*
A human is the most highly developed of the **hominids**. Humans belong to the **genus** *Homo*. Humans appeared about two million years ago, in Africa. One of the first humans was *Homo habilis*. It was small and used tools. *Homo erectus* was a more advanced human which appeared about 1.5 million years ago. Modern humans, *Homo sapiens*, appeared about 100,000 years ago.

hunter-gatherer *noun*
A hunter-gatherer is a person who lives from the land. Hunter-gatherers hunt wild animals, catch fish, and gather edible plants and honey, for their food. Human ancestors were hunter-gatherers, until about 11,000 years ago. The Inuit of the Arctic and Aborigines of Australia are still traditionally hunter-gatherers.

Hyaenodon *noun*
Hyaenodon was a member of the **creodont** order of **mammals**. It lived in the **Eocene** and **Miocene Epochs**, in Europe, North America and Asia. *Hyaenodon* had sharp **canine** teeth for eating flesh and grew to about two metres long.

Hylaeosaurus *noun*
Hylaeosaurus was a **dinosaur** from the **Cretaceous Period**. It belonged to the **ankylosaur** group. Like other ankylosaurs, its body and tail were heavily armoured with bony plates and spikes. *Hylaeosaurus* reached about four metres in length. It was the first **nodosaurid** to be discovered.

Hylonomus *noun*
Hylonomus is one of the earliest **reptiles** so far discovered. It was very much like living lizards, and grew to about 20 centimetres in length. *Hylonomus* fed on insects and other invertebrates.

Hyperodapedon *noun*
Hyperodapedon was a **reptile** which lived in the **Triassic Period**. It was a member of the **rhynchosaur** group. *Hyperodapedon* was about two metres long, and had short legs, like a large lizard. *Hyperodapedon* had strong, bony jaws with which it tore off its plant food.

Hypsilophodon *noun*
Hypsilophodon was a **dinosaur** from the **Cretaceous Period**. It belonged to the **ornithopod** group and was about two metres long. *Hypsilophodon* had a bird-like beak instead of front teeth.

Hyracotherium *noun*
Hyracotherium is the earliest known **horse**. It lived in the **Eocene Epoch**. *Hyracotherium* is sometimes known by the name *Eohippus*. It was a small animal, about 30 centimetres in height. Unlike modern horses, *Hyracotherium* had toes on its feet, not hooves. It was a browser, nibbling leaves from shrubs in swampy forests. It probably had a striped coat to act as camouflage.

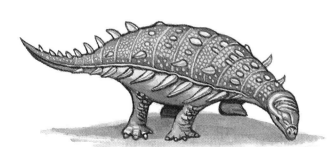

hominid evolution *noun*

Hominid evolution describes how humans developed over millions of years. ***Australopithecus*** was the earliest **hominid**. Some hominids that lived in prehistoric times are now extinct. Several different species of *Australopithecus* have been identified, including **Nutcracker man**. As time went by, hominids developed large brains. They learned to make tools, grow their own food, and lived in permanent settlements.

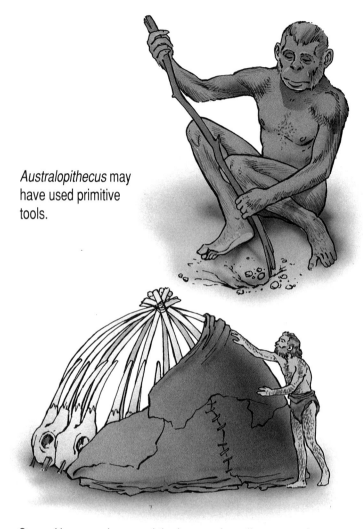

Australopithecus may have used primitive tools.

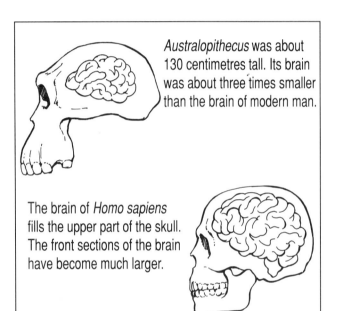

Australopithecus was about 130 centimetres tall. Its brain was about three times smaller than the brain of modern man.

The brain of *Homo sapiens* fills the upper part of the skull. The front sections of the brain have become much larger.

Some *Homo sapiens* used the bones of woolly mammoths to make their tents.

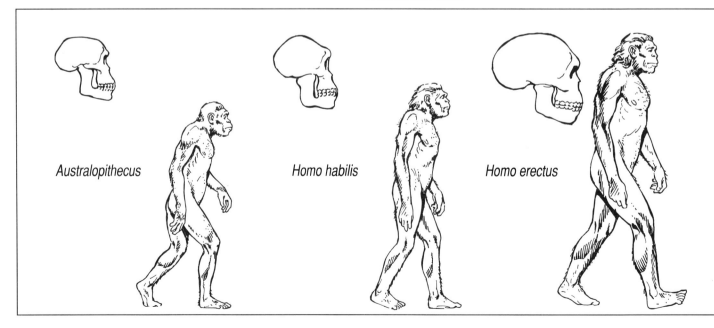

Australopithecus   *Homo habilis*   *Homo erectus*

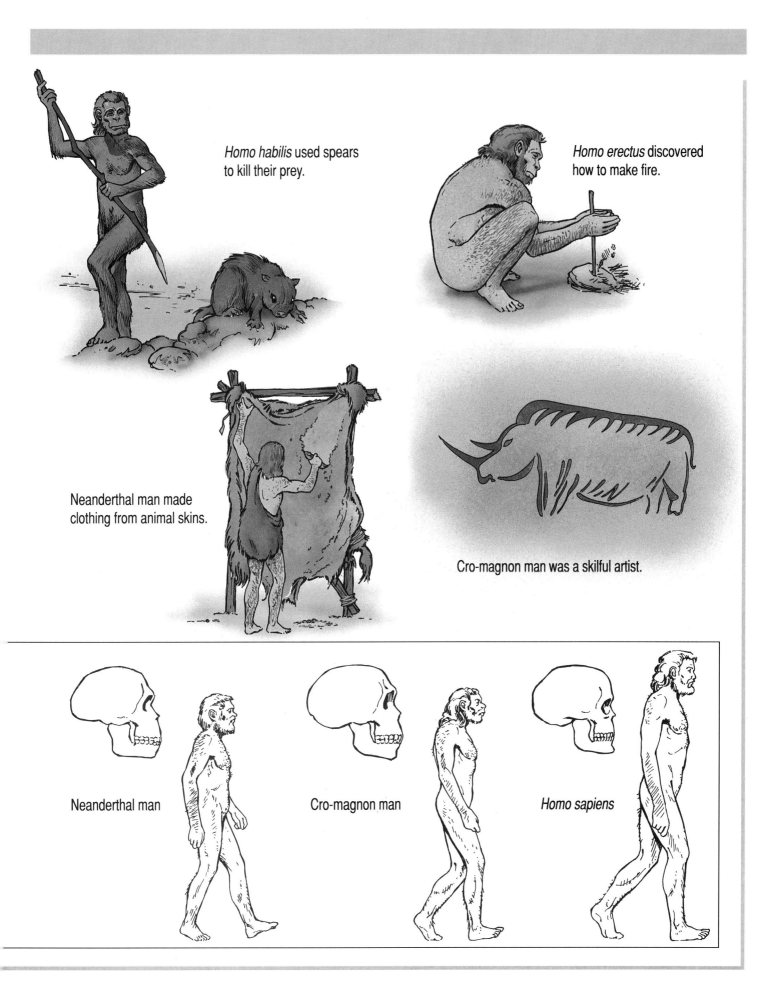

Homo habilis used spears to kill their prey.

Homo erectus discovered how to make fire.

Neanderthal man made clothing from animal skins.

Cro-magnon man was a skilful artist.

Neanderthal man

Cro-magnon man

Homo sapiens

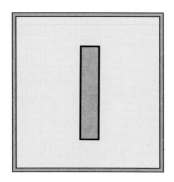

Icaronycteris   *noun*
Icaronycteris was a **bat** which lived in the
Eocene Epoch. Bats probably evolved from
some ground-living **insectivore**.
Icaronycteris was the earliest known bat, but
was already fully developed as a flying
mammal. *Icaronycteris* probably caught
insects in flight.

Ice Age   *noun*
An Ice Age is a period of many centuries
when the climate is cold. During an Ice Age,
ice sheets and glaciers cover large areas of
the Earth. The most recent Ice Age began
about 15,000 years ago and ended about
10,000 years ago.

ichnite   *noun*
An ichnite is a kind of **fossil**. It is a **trace
fossil** of a track or **footprint** left by an
animal.

ichnology   *noun*
Ichnology is the study of traces. It includes
the study of **trace fossils** and of the tracks
made by living animals. An ichnologist is a
person who studies ichnology.

Ichthyornis   *noun*
Ichthyornis was a **bird** which lived in the
Cretaceous Period. It looked like
Hesperornis, but was smaller, and had fully
developed wings. It was the first bird to have
a strong breastbone which provided an
anchor for the wing-flapping muscles. Like
Hesperornis, it had teeth in its jaws.
Ichthyornis probably lived rather like a
seagull.

ichthyosaur   *noun*
An ichthyosaur was an aquatic reptile. The
ichthyosaur group lived from the **Triassic**
until the **Cretaceous Periods**. Ichthyosaurs
were dolphin shaped, with paddle-like
flippers and a fin on their back. They lived in
the sea. Ichthyosaurs had sharp teeth and
fed mostly on fish.

Ichthyosaurus   *noun*
Ichthyosaurus was an **ichthyosaur** which
lived in the **Jurassic Period**. Its fossils have
been found in Europe and Greenland.
Ichthyosaurus grew to about two metres
long and swam fast in search of fish.

Ichthyostega   *noun*
Ichthyostega was a very early **amphibian**.
It lived in the **Devonian Period**.
Ichthyostega was about one metre long and
lived in water and on land. It could walk
slowly with a twisting movement, like a
salamander. *Ichthyostega* probably fed on
fish and other aquatic animals.

Iguanodon   *noun*
Iguanodon was one of the first **dinosaurs** to
be discovered, in 1825. It belonged to the
ornithopod group and lived during the
Cretaceous Period. *Iguanodon* was about
10 metres long. It was probably very
common as many **skeletons** have been
found in Europe, Asia and Africa.

insect *noun*

An insect is an **invertebrate** that has six legs. Many insects also have wings and feelers, or antennae. The first insects were wingless. They appeared early in the **Devonian Period**. Some early insects had wings that did not fold. This made it difficult to escape from a predator. Insects gradually became more numerous and more varied as more kinds of plant developed. Not many insects were preserved as **fossils**, as their bodies rotted away quickly.

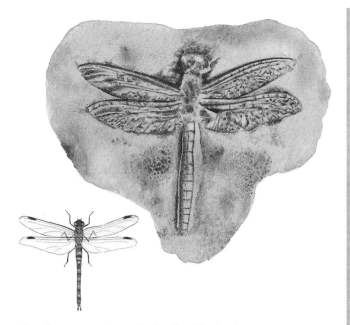

Petalura was a dragonfly that lived by fresh water.

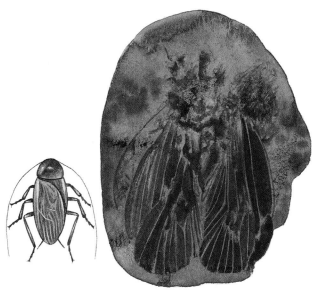

Archimylacris was a cockroach with folding wings. It lived in the late Carboniferous Period.

This sweat bee was trapped in a sticky tree resin called copal.

Bibio was a fly with only one pair of wings. It lived in the Pliocene Epoch.

igneous rock   *noun*
An igneous rock is a kind of **rock** formed from molten material. Igneous rocks form deep inside the Earth. Sometimes, they form at the surface, perhaps in volcanoes. The other main kinds of rock are **sedimentary rock** and **metamorphic rock**.

ilium   *noun*
An ilium is a **bone**. It is one of the three bones making up the **hip** of a **vertebrate** animal. The other bones of the hip are the **pubis** and **ischium**.

incisor   *noun*
An incisor is a kind of **tooth**. Incisors are the front teeth. In most **mammals**, the incisors are flat and rather thin. They are used to bite off pieces of food. In **rodents**, the incisors are used for gnawing.

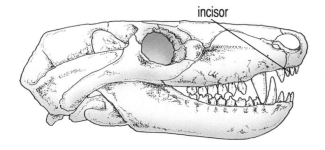

incisor

index fossil   *noun*
An index fossil is a **fossil** which is always found in a particular age of rock. Whenever an index fossil is found, it shows that the rock is of a certain age. Index fossils can be used to date other fossils, by **relative dating**.

Indosuchus   *noun*
Indosuchus was a large **dinosaur** which lived in the **Cretaceous Period**. The remains of *Indosuchus* have been found in India. It belonged to the **carnosaur** group. *Indosuchus* was about six metres long and had long, sharp teeth. It fed mainly on other dinosaurs.

insect ► page 75

insectivore   *noun*
An insectivore is an animal which feeds mainly on **insects**. Anteaters, hedgehogs and shrews are examples of insectivores. The insectivores also form oné of the **orders** of **mammals**.

interglacial   *noun*
An interglacial is a warm period between two **glaciations**. During an interglacial, the temperature is higher than during the glaciations which come before and after it. The last interglacial was the Ipswichian which ended about 64,000 years ago.

invertebrate   *noun*
Invertebrates are many-celled animals without backbones. Sponges, jellyfish, starfish, molluscs and arthropods are examples of invertebrates. There are about 1.3 million species of invertebrate known today. Some invertebrates, such as **trilobites**, **ammonites** and **graptolites**, are extinct. They can only be studied from **fossils**.

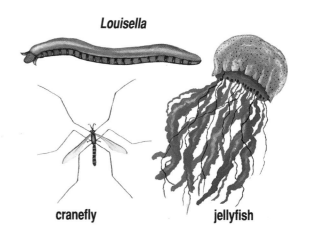

Louisella

cranefly   jellyfish

iridium   *noun*
Iridium is a chemical element. It is found in large quantities in meteorites. Iridium is also found in some **rocks** dated at around the time of the **extinction** of the **dinosaurs**. Because of this, some scientists think that their extinction may have been caused by a huge meteorite colliding with the Earth.

Irish elk ► **Megaloceros**

Iron Age   *noun*
The Iron Age was a time in human history. It was around 3,000 years ago. In the Iron Age, people first learned how to smelt iron and make iron tools.

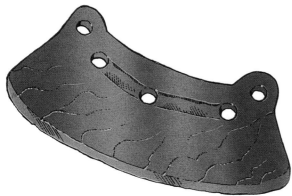

iron razor made about 2,500 years ago

iron pyrite   *noun*
Iron pyrite is a mineral. It is very shiny and contains crystals. Iron pyrite contains iron and sulphur. It has a gold colour and is sometimes called 'fool's gold'.

ischium   *noun*
The ischium is a bone. It is one of the three bones making up the **hip** of a **vertebrate** animal. The other bones of the hip are the **pubis** and **ilium**.

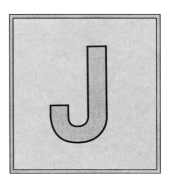

jawless fish ► **agnathan**

jaws   *noun*
Jaws are a part of an animal. They are hard mouthparts, specialized for biting or catching prey. Because the jaws of **vertebrates** and the teeth they contain are so hard, they are often preserved as **fossils**.

jellyfish   *noun*
Jellyfish are **invertebrate** animals. They belong to the coelenterate **phylum**. Fossil jellyfish are rare because their soft bodies do not preserve well. Most fossil jellyfish are **trace fossils**. Jellyfish first appeared in the **Precambrian Period**.

Jurassic Period ► page 72

Jurassic Period *noun*

The Jurassic was a time in **geological history**. The Jurassic Period lasted from about 213 million years ago to about 144 million years ago. The **dinosaurs** ruled the land during the Jurassic Period. Many of the dinosaurs grew to an enormous size. The first true **bird**, *Archaeopteryx*, evolved, and many kinds of crocodile developed. **Conifers** were common in the Jurassic Period.

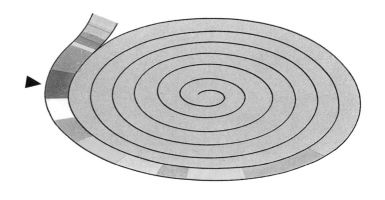

The arrow shows where the Jurassic Period lies in relation to the geological history of the Earth.

1. *Rhamphorhyncus*
2. *Geosaurus*
3. *Icthyosaurus*
4. *Cryptocleidus*
5. *Protosuchus*
6. *Ultrasaurus*
7. *Stegosaurus*
8. *Fabrosaurus*
9. *Archaeopteryx*
10. ammonite

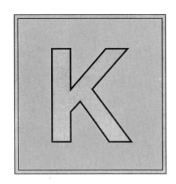

Kamptobaatar *noun*

Kamptobaatar was a small **mammal**. It lived during the **Cretaceous Period**, and its skeletons have been found in Mongolia. *Kamptobaatar* was only about the size of a mouse. Its teeth show that it must have fed on plants or their seeds.

Kannemeyeria *noun*

Kannemeyeria was a mammal-like **reptile**. It lived in the **Triassic Period**, and its remains have been found in India and Africa. *Kannemeyeria* was about three metres long and had a fat body, a little like a hippopotamus. It fed on plants, which it crushed in its horny jaws.

kieselguhr *noun*

Kieselguhr is a kind of mud. It is formed from millions of diatoms, and is often called diatomite. When diatoms die, their hard cell walls gather on the bed of the sea or lake. Under some conditions, layer after layer gathers there, forming kieselguhr. Kieselguhr is mined for use in filters or for polishing.

Kosmoceras *noun*

Kosmoceras was an **ammonite**. It lived in the **Jurassic Period**. Fossils of *Kosmoceras* have been found all over the world. It was about six centimetres across and swam in the seas.

Kronosaurus *noun*

Kronosaurus was a marine **reptile** which lived in the **Cretaceous Period**. It belonged to the **plesiosaur** group. *Kronosaurus* was about 17 metres long.

Kuehneosaurus *noun*

Kuehneosaurus was a small **reptile** which lived in the **Triassic Period**. It had remarkably long ribs sticking out from the side of its body. *Kuehneosaurus* could spread out these ribs and glide through the air on the skin stretched between them.

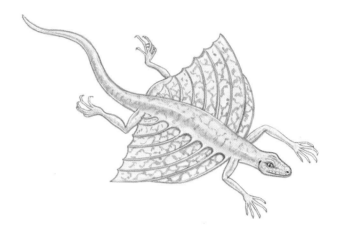

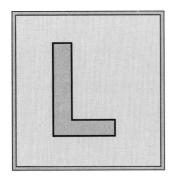

labyrinthodont   *noun*
A labyrinthodont was an **amphibian**. The labyrinthodonts lived in the **Paleozoic Era** and the **Triassic Period**. Some labyrinthodonts were very large, up to several metres long. **Reptiles** probably evolved from the labyrinthodonts.

Lambeosaurus   *noun*
Lambeosaurus was a large **dinosaur** from the **Cretaceous Period**. It was a duck-billed dinosaur, or **hadrosaur**, and belonged to the **ornithopod** group. *Lambeosaurus* reached about 15 metres long. It had a large, bony crest on the top of its head.

Lascaux Caves   *noun*
The Lascaux Caves are a series of caves with ancient paintings on their walls. They are in France, in the Dordogne region. This **cave art** dates from the **Paleolithic Period** of human history and is between about 15,000 and 17,000 years old. The paintings in the Lascaux Caves include clear, coloured pictures of the **aurochs**.

Latimeria ► coelacanth

Laurasia   *noun*
Laurasia is the name of a large continent. It formed when the super-continent of **Pangaea** split about 150 million years ago, during the **Mesozoic Era**. Laurasia gradually split further, to create North America, Greenland, Europe and Asia.

Lepidodendron
noun
Lepidodendron was a giant club moss. It grew in the **Carboniferous Period** and has been found all over the world. *Lepidodendron* reached 40 metres in height and had a straight trunk with grass-like leaves spreading from its crown. It grew in hot, swampy areas.

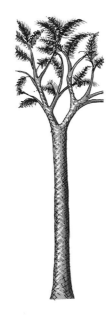

lepidosaur   *noun*
The lepidosaurs are a group of **diapsid reptiles**. They include **lizards**, **tuataras** and **snakes**. The lepidosaurs first appeared during the late **Paleozoic Era**.

Lepidotus   *noun*
Lepidotus was a fish. It lived in the **Mesozoic Era** and grew to nearly two metres in length. *Lepidotus* lived in shallow water and fed on invertebrates. It could crush shells with its hard teeth. *Lepidotus* had rows of large, square scales, which preserve well as **fossils**.

Lesothosaurus   *noun*
Lesothosaurus was a small **dinosaur** from the **Triassic Period**. It was only about 90 centimetres long and looked like a long-legged lizard. *Lesothosaurus* lived in dry, desert areas and its remains have been found in southern Africa. It was a **herbivore**.

Leuciscus *noun*
Leuciscus is a small bony fish which is found in North America, Asia and Africa. It is also known as a dace. *Leuciscus* lives in freshwater streams and lakes, feeding on plants. It is about nine centimetres in length, with a long, silvery body and no teeth. *Leuciscus* first appeared during the **Oligocene Epoch**.

Lexovisaurus *noun*
Lexovisaurus was a **dinosaur** which lived in the **Jurassic Period**. It belonged to the **stegosaur** group. It was a little smaller than *Stegosaurus*, reaching about five metres in length.*Lexovisaurus* had flat, horny armour plates sticking out from its neck, back and tail.

lignite *noun*
Lignite, or brown coal, is a kind of **coal**. It has a brown colour and burns with a very smoky flame. Lignite contains about 65 per cent carbon, which is much less than coal. It has more carbon than peat, but less than anthracite.

limestone *noun*
Limestone is a **sedimentary rock**. It usually has a grainy texture. Limestone often contains shells of marine animals and organisms such as **foraminiferans**. **Fossils** are commonly found in limestone.

Lingula *noun*
Lingula is a **brachiopod**. It lives in burrows in sand which is regularly covered by the sea. *Lingula* grows to about 1.5 centimetres long. Fossils of *Lingula* date back as far as the **Cambrian Period**. A living *Lingula* is very similar to the fossils.

Liopleurodon *noun*
Liopleurodon was a marine **reptile** which lived in the **Jurassic Period**. It belonged to the **plesiosaur** family. *Liopleurodon* grew to about 10 metres long and had a large head with a short neck. Its limbs were like paddles and it fed on fish and **belemnites**.

living fossil *noun*
A living fossil is an animal or plant which is still found today, but which is similar to ancient **fossils**. Examples of living fossils are the **coelacanth**, the **tuatara**, *Lingula* and the **swamp cypress**, or *Metasequoia*.

lizard *noun*
A lizard is a kind of **reptile**. Most lizards have four short limbs and a long tail. Lizards are **diapsid** reptiles. They belong to the **lepidosaur** group which also includes **tuataras** and **snakes**. Lizards first appeared during the late **Jurassic Period**.

lizard-footed dinosaur ► sauropod

lizard-hipped dinosaur ► saurischian

lobe-finned fish ► sarcopterygian

Lufengosaurus *noun*
Lufengosaurus was a **dinosaur** from China. It lived in the early **Jurassic Period**. *Lufengosaurus* belonged to the **prosauropod** group. It grew to about six metres in length and had a long tail and neck.

lung *noun*
A lung is an organ which is used for breathing air. Mammals, birds, reptiles and most adult amphibians have lungs. The first animals to develop lungs were early bony fish. Some of the **placoderms** may also have had lungs. Land-living **vertebrates** use their lungs to take in **oxygen** from the air.

lycopod *noun*

The lycopods, or club mosses, are a group of plants. They belong to the **pteridophytes**. Lycopods are moss-like plants. They have scale-like leaves which grow in a spiral on the stem. Some lycopods produce cones. Lycopods first appeared in the **Devonian Period**. Today's lycopods are small, low-growing plants, but in the **Carboniferous Period** there were giant lycopods which reached 35 metres in height.

Lystrosaurus *noun*

Lystrosaurus was a **reptile** from the **Triassic Period**. It belonged to the **therapsid** group. *Lystrosaurus* was about two metres long. It had a rather short tail and stumpy legs. It probably fed on plants which it tore with its heavy, wide jaws.

machairodont *noun*

A machairodont was one of a group of cats. The machairodonts were the sabre-toothed cats which lived in the **Miocene** and **Pliocene Epochs**. They had very long upper canine teeth, which they used as daggers. Machairodonts included *Homotherium* in Europe and ***Smilodon*** in America.

Macrophalangia *noun*

Macrophalangia was a **dinosaur** which lived in the late **Cretaceous Period**. It was a **theropod** and had four long, slender toes on each foot. Fossils of *Macrophalangia* have been found in North America.

Magnolia *noun*

Magnolia is a **genus** of flowering plant. It is one of the earliest known of all flowering plants. Fossil pollen and leaves of *Magnolia* date back to the **Cretaceous Period**. Many kinds of *Magnolia* still grow today. Their flowers are made up in much the same way as the early forms.

mammal   *noun*

A mammal is a **vertebrate** animal. Mammals have hair on their body and have four limbs. Female mammals usually give birth to live young, and feed the young on milk from their bodies. Scientists divide mammals into three groups. The three groups are placental mammals, marsupials and monotremes. Mammals first evolved in the **Triassic Period** about 220 million years ago. The first mammals were small, nocturnal insectivores. After the dinosaurs became extinct at the end of the Cretaceous Period, mammals started to evolve into many different forms.

marsupial

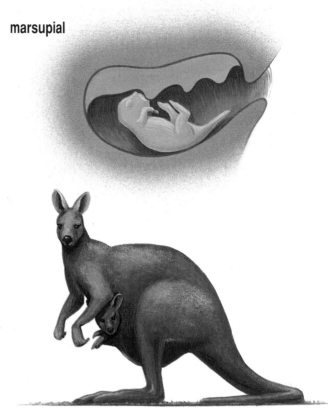

Marsupials such as the kangaroo give birth to a tiny, helpless offspring. The young makes its way to the mother's pouch where it attaches itself to a teat. It stays in the pouch until its development is complete.

placental mammal

Young placental mammals, such as rabbits, develop in the mother's body. They are fed by an organ called the placenta. After they are born, they feed on milk from the mother's body.

monotreme

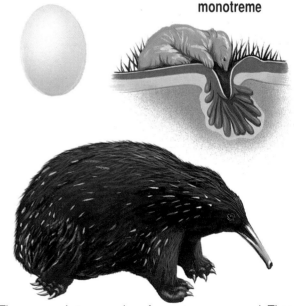

There are only two species of monotreme mammal. These are the echidna and the platypus. The monotremes have no teeth, and they lay eggs. When young echidna hatch, they feed on milk that oozes from the mother's body.

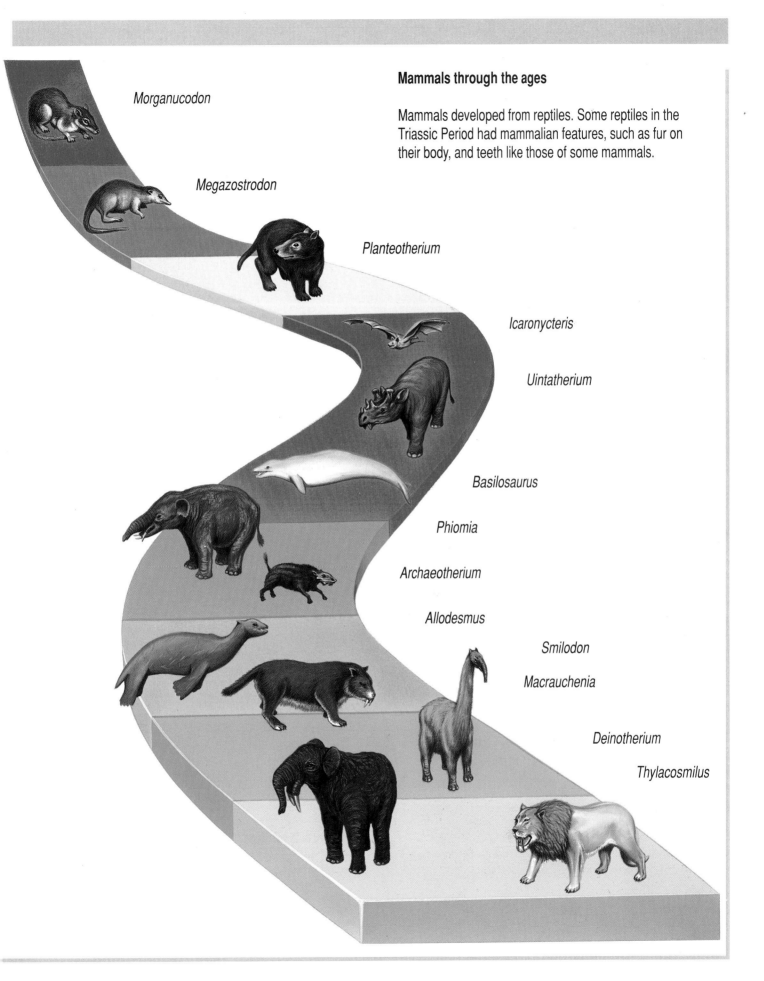

Morganucodon

Megazostrodon

Planteotherium

Mammals through the ages

Mammals developed from reptiles. Some reptiles in the Triassic Period had mammalian features, such as fur on their body, and teeth like those of some mammals.

Icaronycteris

Uintatherium

Basilosaurus

Phiomia

Archaeotherium

Allodesmus

Smilodon

Macrauchenia

Deinotherium

Thylacosmilus

Maiasaura   *noun*
Maiasaura was a **dinosaur** from the
Cretaceous Period. It belonged to the
ornithopod group and grew to about nine
metres long. *Maiasaura* skeletons were
found together with their nests, eggs and
hatchlings. The young that were found were
about one metre long, but they were not
freshly hatched. This shows that dinosaurs
may have looked after their young after
hatching. *Maiasaura* means 'good mother
reptile'.

Mamenchisaurus   *noun*
Mamenchisaurus was a large **dinosaur** that
lived in the **Jurassic Period**. It belonged to
the **sauropod** group. *Mamenchisaurus* had
a very long neck and tail and reached about
27 metres long, about half of which was its
neck. Like the other sauropods,
Mamenchisaurus lived on land.

mammal ▶ page 84

mammal-footed ▶ **theropod**

mammal-like reptile ▶ **therosaur**

mammoth   *noun*
A mammoth was a large **mammal** which
lived many thousands of years ago during
the **Pleistocene Epoch**. Mammoths are
now extinct. They died out about 10,000
years ago. Like modern elephants,
mammoths had long tusks and trunks, but
their hair was much thicker, and reddish in
colour. They are also known as woolly
mammoths. Mammoths are sometimes
found frozen in ice in very cold regions.

Mammut   *noun*
Mammut was a relative of the elephant.
It lived in North America from the **Miocene
Epoch** until the **Pleistocene Epoch**. It is
also called a **mastodon**. *Mammut* was
about 2.5 metres tall at the shoulder. It may
have lived partly in water, and partly in the
forests.

Mammuthus   *noun*
Mammuthus was a kind of elephant which
lived in the **Pleistocene Epoch**. It is also
known as a **mammoth**. Its skeletons have
been found in Africa, Asia and Europe.
The largest kinds of *Mammuthus* were the
biggest elephants that have ever lived, some
reaching four metres tall at the shoulder.
Mammuthus had thick, reddish fur and huge,
upturned tusks. Whole bodies of
Mammuthus have been dug up from the
frozen soils of Siberia. *Mammuthus* features
in some **cave art**.

man ▶ **human**

Mariopteris   *noun*
Mariopteris was a **seedfern**. It lived in the
Carboniferous and **Permian Periods**.
Fossils of *Mariopteris* leaves are often found
in coal. In life, it grew to about five metres
tall, in swampy areas. Like other seedferns,
Mariopteris had feathery, fern-like leaves.

marsupial   *noun*
A marsupial is one of a group of **mammals**.
Unlike most mammals, baby marsupials are
born very early in their development. They
spend the first part of their life in their
mother's pouch. There are about 250
species of marsupial, mainly in Australia and
South America. The marsupials first
appeared in the late **Cretaceous Period**, in
North America, but became extinct there.
They appeared in Australia in the **Miocene
Epoch**.

mass-extinction *noun*
A mass-extinction describes what happens when many species of plant or animal become extinct together over a short period of time. For example, the **dinosaurs** suffered a mass-extinction towards the end of the **Cretaceous Period**.

mastodon ► **Mammut**

megalith *noun*
A megalith is a huge stone in a monument built by early people. Many megaliths are found in north-west Europe, at sites such as **Carnac** in France, and **Stonehenge** in England. Megaliths were probably moved by pushing them on rolling tree trunks.

Megaloceros *noun*
Megaloceros was a large deer which lived in the **Pleistocene Epoch**. It is also called the Irish elk, or Irish deer. Remains of *Megaloceros* have been found in many parts of Europe and Asia. The male *Megaloceros* had huge antlers, up to three metres across.

Megalosaurus *noun*
Megalosaurus was a **dinosaur** which lived in the **Jurassic** and early **Cretaceous Periods**. It belonged to the **carnosaur** group, and was a fierce predator. *Megalosaurus* was the first dinosaur to be named, in 1824. It grew to about nine metres in length.

Megatherium *noun*
Megatherium was a giant sloth. It lived in South America in the **Pliocene** and **Pleistocene Epochs**. It was the size of an elephant, about six metres long and three metres high at the shoulder. Although fierce-looking, *Megatherium* probably fed on leaves. *Megatherium* became extinct only about 10,000 years ago and its bones have been found in caves.

Megazostrodon *noun*
Megazostrodon was an early form of **mammal**. It lived in the late **Jurassic Period**. It was a small **insectivore**, about the size and shape of a shrew. *Megazostrodon* was probably nocturnal and preyed on small invertebrates.

Merychippus *noun*
Merychippus was an early form of horse. It lived in North America, during the **Miocene Epoch**. *Merychippus* was about the size of a modern pony. *Merychippus* had long legs and could run fast. It lived on the open plains and fed mainly on grasses.

Merycoidodon *noun*
Merycoidodon was a **mammal**. It was a sheep-like grass-eater, or ruminant, which was common in North America. *Merycoidodon* lived in the **Oligocene** and **Miocene Epochs**. It moved about in herds in wooded and open country, feeding on grasses and other plants.

Miocene Epoch *noun*

The Miocene Epoch was a time in **geological history**. It lasted from about 24.5 million to about 5 million years ago. The plant life of the Miocene Epoch looked much like modern vegetation. There were many different kinds of mammal, including early elephants, horses, bears and rhinoceroses. **Marsupials** could travel between Australasia and South America because the two continents were still joined together as Gondwana.

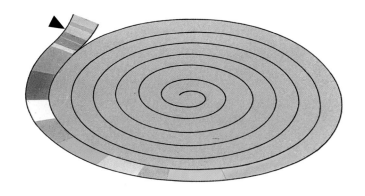

The arrow shows where the Miocene Epoch lies in relation to the geological history of the Earth.

1. *Proconsul*
2. *Deinotherium*
3. *Epigaulus*
4. *Alticamelus*
5. *Barbourofelis*
6. *Synthetoceras*
7. *Phorusrhacus*
8. *Coelodonta*
9. *Hypohippus*

Mesohippus *noun*
Mesohippus was an early form of horse.
It lived in North America in the **Oligocene Epoch**. *Mesohippus* had three toes on each foot, not hooves like horses today. It was a woodland **browser**.

Mesolithic *adjective*
Mesolithic describes an archaeological period. It is also called the Middle Stone Age. The Mesolithic period was between about 10,000 and 4,000 years ago.

mesosaur *noun*
A mesosaur was one of a group of **anapsid reptiles**. The mesosaurs lived in the **Carboniferous** and **Permian Periods**. Mesosaurs were aquatic. They had a flattened tail, short limbs and a long snout. Some mesosaurs had fine, needle-like teeth. They may have used these to filter tiny crustaceans from the water, as food.

Mesozoic Era *noun*
The Mesozoic Era is one of the divisions of **geological history**. It lasted from about 245 million years ago until about 65 million years ago. The first **mammals** and **birds** appeared in the Mesozoic Era.

Metasequoia ► **swamp cypress**

Metriorhynchus *noun*
Metriorhynchus was a crocodile. It lived in the **Jurassic Period**. *Metriorhynchus* grew to about three metres long. Unlike living crocodiles, it spent all or nearly all its life in the sea. It had a fish-like tail to help it swim. *Metriorhynchus* fed on fish and cephalopods.

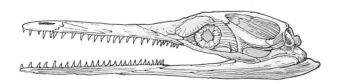

Micraster *noun*
Micraster is an extinct sea urchin. It lived in the upper **Cretaceous Period**. *Micraster* is known as a heart urchin because of its heart-shaped skeleton. It lived in chalky sea-beds, and its fossils are found in chalk.

millipede *noun*
A millipede is a shiny **arthropod** which has many pairs of legs. There are about 10,000 species of millipede, mostly found in tropical countries. The body of a millipede is divided into segments, and each segment has two pairs of legs. Some millipedes have as many as 240 pairs of legs, but most have fewer than 100 pairs. Most millipedes eat plants and dead leaves, although some are carnivores. Millipedes first appeared in the **Silurian Period**.

mineralization *noun*
Mineralization is one of the processes which produce a **fossil**. Mineral salts enter the remains of a body and change their chemical make-up. This makes the fossil last longer in the soil or rock.

Miocene Epoch ► page 88

Mississippian Epoch *noun*
The Mississippian Epoch was a time in **geological history**. The Mississippian Epoch is the earlier part of the **Carboniferous Period**. It lasted from about 360 million to about 300 million years ago. In Europe, the Mississippian Epoch is called the Lower Carboniferous Period.

Mixosaurus *noun*

Mixosaurus was an **aquatic reptile**. It lived in the **Triassic Period**, in shallow seas. *Mixosaurus* belonged to the **ichthyosaur** group. It had a body like a dolphin, with flippers instead of legs, and a fish-like tail and fins. *Mixosaurus* was about 1.2 metres long. It had a beak with many small teeth and fed on fish.

moa ► **Dinornis**

Moeritherium *noun*

Moeritherium was an early kind of elephant. It lived in the **Eocene** and **Oligocene Epochs**, in Africa. It was about one metre tall and had short tusks, but no trunk.

molar *noun*

A molar is a kind of **tooth**. Molars are the flat-topped teeth towards the back of the mouth. They are used for grinding food. **Herbivores** have well-developed molars for chewing up tough grasses and other plants.

mollusc ► page 92

Monograptus *noun*

Monograptus was an extinct kind of **invertebrate** animal called a **graptolite**. It lived in the **Silurian** and **Devonian Periods**, floating in open seas. Fossils of *Monograptus* are often a gentle spiral shape, up to 20 centimetres across.

monotreme *adjective*

Monotreme describes an unusual kind of **mammal** which lays eggs and has no teeth. There are only three species of monotreme mammal alive today. These are the duck-billed platypus and the two kinds of echidna, or spiny anteater. They live in Australasia. Young monotreme mammals feed on their mother's milk after hatching from the eggs. Monotreme mammals first appeared in the **Cretaceous Period**.

Morganucodon *noun*

Morganucodon is one of the earliest known **mammals**. It was a mouse-like animal which lived in the **Triassic Period**. Like most mammals, it had fur. But it probably laid eggs, like **monotreme mammals**. *Morganucodon* had large eyes and sharp teeth. It probably hunted insects at night.

Moropus *noun*

Moropus was a **mammal** which lived in the late **Oligocene** and early **Miocene Epochs**. It was an **ungulate**, and belonged to the **chalicothere** family. It had a horse-like body, but its feet had claws.

Mosasaurus *noun*

Mosasaurus was an **aquatic reptile**. It lived in the **Cretaceous Period**. *Mosasaurus* was very large, reaching 15 metres long, and had powerful jaws with sharp teeth. These were so strong they could even crush the shells of ammonites. It had a long tail and its limbs were paddles.

mollusc   *noun*

A mollusc is a soft-bodied **invertebrate** with a hard shell. Many kinds of mollusc appeared in the **Cambrian Period**. There are three main **classes** of mollusc. Molluscs with hinged shells are known as **bivalves**. Snails are **gastropods**, and octopuses, squids and ammonites are **cephalopods**.

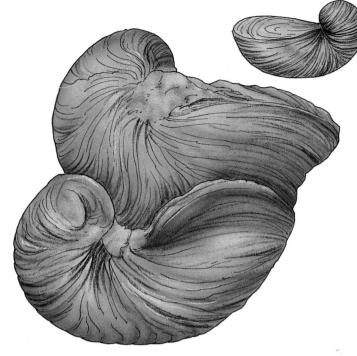

Gryphaea was a bivalve that lived on muddy sea-beds. It is also called the Devil's Toenail.

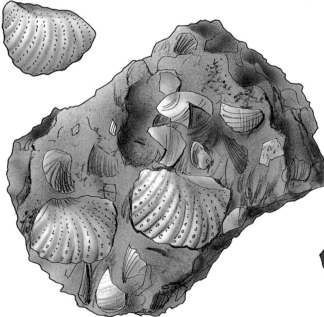

Myophorella was a clam that lived in the seas of the Mesozoic Era.

Dentalium's body was an open-ended tube. The animal's head and foot came out of the larger end.

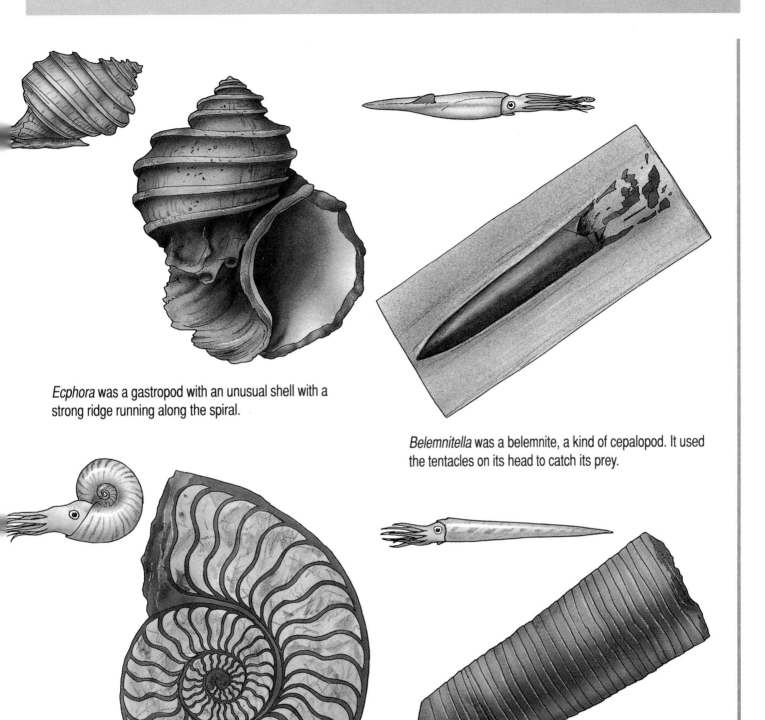

Ecphora was a gastropod with an unusual shell with a strong ridge running along the spiral.

Belemnitella was a belemnite, a kind of cepalopod. It used the tentacles on its head to catch its prey.

Oxynoticeras was an ammonite. It was probably one of the fastest-swimming of all ammonites.

Orthoceras was a cephalopod called a nautiloid. The shell of a nautiloid is divided into small chambers.

Moschops *noun*
Moschops was a mammal-like **reptile** from the **Permian Period**. It had a heavy body with short legs, and reached a length of around three metres. Fossils of *Moschops* have been found in Russia and South Africa.

mudstone *noun*
Mudstone is a kind of **sedimentary rock**. It is made of clay and silt. **Fossils** are often preserved in mudstone.

muscle *noun*
Muscle is a kind of body tissue. The cells inside muscles can become shorter, or contract, so that the muscles change in length. Animals use muscles to move their limbs and support their body. Unlike **bone**, muscle does not preserve or fossilize well.

nautiloid *noun*
A nautiloid is a **mollusc**, in the same family as octopuses. Nautiloids belong to the **cephalopod** group and live in the sea. They have a heavy, coiled shell. The shells of extinct nautiloids are often found as **fossils**. Nautiloids feed on fish and are thought to rest in coral crevices during the day and to swim at night. They were most common in the **Paleozoic Era**. *Orthoceras* and *Huronia* are examples of fossil nautiloids.

Neanderthal people *noun*
Neanderthal people were a form of the human species, ***Homo sapiens***. They lived in Europe during the cold climate of the last Ice Ages, from about 100,000 years ago. Neanderthal people had a large brain, but a heavier body than modern people. They became extinct about 35,000 years ago. Neanderthal people used fire, hunted animals for food and buried their dead. They wore thick clothes made from animal skins to protect them from the cold.

neck *noun*
A neck is the part of an animal's body between the head and the shoulders. It contains the top vertebrae of the spine which support the head. A neck may be short and thick, as in cattle, or long and thin, as in many **dinosaurs**.

Neogene *noun*
The Neogene is a time in **geological history**. It is a division of the **Tertiary Period**. The Neogene is made up of the **Miocene** and **Pliocene Epochs**.

Neolithic *adjective*
Neolithic describes an archaeological **period**. The Neolithic period lasted from about 4,000 until about 2,500 years ago. Neolithic people used stone tools. The Neolithic period is sometimes called the New Stone Age.

nest *noun*
A nest is a place prepared by an animal for its eggs or young. By keeping its young in a nest, an animal can help protect them from enemies. Sometimes, **dinosaur** nests have been found with eggs inside.

Nipa *noun*
Nipa is a **genus** of palm. It is also known as the stemless palm because it has little or no stem. It has long leaves which grow up from close to the ground. *Nipa* produces fruits which look like coconuts. It grows in mangrove swamps in South-east Asia. Fossils of *Nipa* have been found dating back to the **Cretaceous Period**.

Nipponites *noun*
Nipponites was an **ammonite**. Its fossils, dating from the **Cretaceous Period**, have been found in Japan and North America. *Nipponites* was one of the strangest ammonites. Its shell was twisted into a series of U shapes and was about five centimetres across. *Nipponites* probably lived drifting in the warm surface waters of the sea. It fed on small animals which it caught with its tentacles.

Noasaurus *noun*
Noasaurus was a **dinosaur** which lived in the **Cretaceous Period**. Its remains have been found in South America. Like *Deinonychus*, *Noasaurus* had a special, large, hooked claw on each foot, with which it attacked its prey. *Noasaurus* was about 2.5 metres long.

nocturnal *adjective*
Nocturnal describes an animal which is active at night. The opposite of nocturnal is diurnal. Many **mammals** are nocturnal, and so are some **birds**, such as owls and nightjars. There are also millions of nocturnal **insects**, particularly in the tropics. Most nocturnal animals can see and hear very well.

non-flowering plant ► **gymnosperm**

Notharctus *noun*
Notharctus was a **mammal** which lived in the early **Eocene Epoch**. It was a primate which lived largely in the trees and looked like a lemur. *Notharctus* had a long tail and was able to climb and jump well.

nothosaur *noun*
A nothosaur was one of a group of **reptiles** which lived in the **Triassic Period**. Nothosaurs had a long neck and swam in the sea.

Nothosaurus *noun*
Nothosaurus was an **aquatic reptile** from the **Triassic Period**. It was about six metres long and, like other **nothosaurs**, had a long neck and tail. Its feet were probably webbed.

Nothrotherium   *noun*
Nothrotherium was a **mammal**. It was a kind of sloth which lived in South America and North America during the **Pleistocene Epoch**. *Nothrotherium* was about two metres long and lived at ground level, feeding on twigs, leaves and seeds.

notochord   *noun*
The notochord is a stiff rod in the back of **vertebrate** animals. In most vertebrates, it is replaced by the **backbone** as the animal develops.

Notostylops   *noun*
Notostylops was a **mammal** which lived in the **Eocene Epoch**, in South America. It was about 75 centimetres long. *Notostylops* had flat teeth to grind its plant food.

Nummulites   *noun*
Nummulites is a kind of tiny, one-celled animal called a **foraminiferan**. It is one of the largest, at about 1.5 centimetres across. *Nummulites* lived from the **Paleocene** to **Oligocene Epochs** and was common in the warm **Tethys Sea**.

nutcracker man   *noun*
Nutcracker man is the nickname given to a human fossil which was discovered in Tanzania in 1959. It was a species of ***Australopithecus***, and had very large cheek teeth, which gave it its name. Nutcracker man lived about 1,750,000 years ago, in eastern Africa.

nutrition   *noun*
Nutrition is the process of feeding by animals or plants. In nutrition, chemicals from the food are taken in, or absorbed, by the body, to give energy and to allow growth. There are two main kinds of nutrition — **heterotrophic** and **autotrophic**.

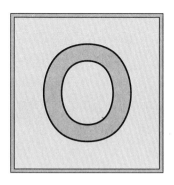

oak *noun*
An oak is a kind of broad-leaved **tree**. It belongs to the **genus** *Quercus*, and is in the same family as beech. There are about 600 species of oak alive today. Oaks include both deciduous and evergreen species. The fruit of an oak is called an acorn. Oaks first appeared during the **Eocene Epoch**.

Odontopteryx *noun*
Odontopteryx was a **bird** which lived in the **Eocene Epoch**. It was a seabird a little like an albatross in shape, with long, narrow wings. *Odontopteryx* had bony teeth to help it to grasp fish.

old red sandstone ► sandstone

oldest living things ► page 98

Olenoides *noun*
Olenoides was a **trilobite** which existed in the **Cambrian Period**. Fossils of *Olenoides* have been found in the **Burgess Shale** deposits. Like other trilobites, *Olenoides* had several pairs of two-branched limbs. It also had feathery limbs for breathing. *Olenoides* lived in the shallow waters of the sea-bed.

Oligocene Epoch ► page 100

omnivore *noun*
An omnivore is an animal which eats a varied diet of animal and plant material. Most **bears** are omnivores, and they eat the meat of other animals and birds, as well as leaves, fruits, nuts, honey and insects.

Ophiderpeton *noun*
Ophiderpeton was an **amphibian** which lived in the **Carboniferous Period**. It had no limbs at all, and looked like a snake. It grew to a length of about 15 centimetres and crawled about in damp soil or in water.

Ophthalmosaurus *noun*
Ophthalmosaurus was an **aquatic reptile** which lived in the **Triassic Period**. It belonged to the **ichthyosaur** group. It was about 3.5 metres long and swam like a large fish. *Ophthalmosaurus* had large eyes and swam quickly after its fish prey.

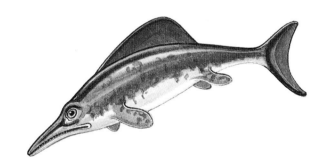

opossum *noun*
An opossum is a **marsupial**. There are about 75 species of opossum, mostly found in South America and Central America. One species also lives in North America, as far north as southern Canada. Opossums are rat-shaped, with a scaly, almost hairless tail and untidy fur. Opossums eat leaves, shoots, buds and seeds, and also insects. They are nocturnal, solitary creatures that mostly live in forests. They first appeared in the **Eocene Epoch**.

oldest living things *plural noun*

The oldest living things lived in the sea. They were simple, single-celled organisms similar to bacteria. Some of these organisms made their food in the same way as plants do. They gave off oxygen which gradually built up in the Earth's atmosphere. For about 2,000 million years, this was the only life on Earth. More complicated cells with a nucleus later developed. The earliest evidence of soft-bodied, **invertebrate** animals is found in **fossils** from the **Precambrian Period**.

A sea pen was probably a kind of soft coral. It attached itself to the sea-bed, and filtered food from the water.

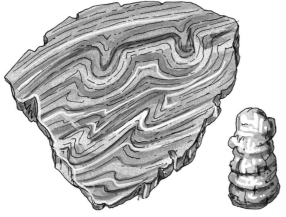

Stromatolites are bun-shaped structures composed of blue-green algae.

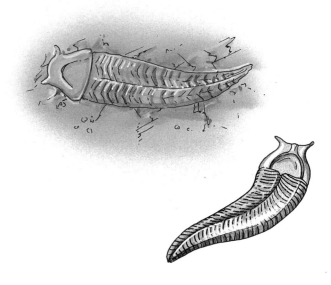

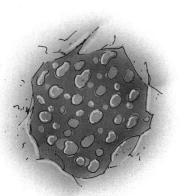

Parka was a green alga dating from the Silurian and Devonian Periods. It was probably a land plant.

Spriggina was a worm-like invertebrate that lived in shallow sea water. Scientists are not sure what group spriggina belongs to.

Many plants and animals are known as living fossils. This is because they have changed very little from the living things that existed millions of years ago.

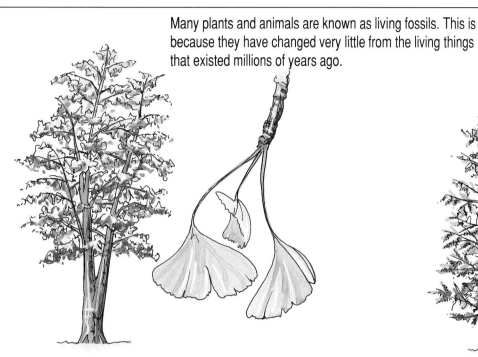

The ginkgo is an unusual tree with fan-shaped leaves. Ginkgo trees first grew in the Permian Period. The natural habitat of the modern ginkgo tree is China.

Pityostrobus was a conifer that was common in the Jurassic and Cretaceous Periods.

The coelacanth is a lobe-finned fish. It was thought to be extinct, but coelacanths have been found living in the seas off the south-east coast of Africa.

The tuatara is the only living species of a group of reptiles. The other species in the group became extinct 140 million years ago. Tuataras live only in New Zealand.

Oligocene Epoch   *noun*

The Oligocene Epoch was a time in **geological history**. The Oligocene Epoch lasted from about 38 million years ago to about 24 million years ago. Large herbivorous mammals grazed on grasses and other low-growing plants. The first apes appeared. Fossils of these early apes have been found in Africa.

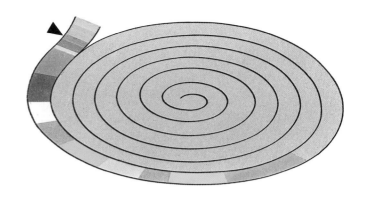

The arrow shows where the Oligocene Epoch lies in relation to the geological history of the Earth.

1. *Brontotherium*
2. *Pyrotherium*
3. *Palaeocastor*
4. *Moropus*
5. *Merycoidodon*
6. *Aegyptopithecus*
7. *Doedicurus*

order *noun*

An order is a rank in the classification of animals and plants. It is the main group between **class** and **family**. For example, the **carnivores** form an order, containing the cat family. The **conifers** are an order, *Coniferales*, within the **gymnosperms**.

Ordovician Period ▶ page 103

organism *noun*

An organism is any living thing. All animals and plants are organisms, and so are fungi, and even microscopic algae and bacteria. All organisms have a body made of cells. They also feed and reproduce. The first organisms appeared in the **Precambrian Era**, about 1,500 million years ago.

ornithischian *noun*

An ornithischian is one of a group of **dinosaurs**. It is a bird-hipped dinosaur. The other group is the **saurischians**, or lizard-hipped dinosaurs. In the ornithischians, the **hip** bones are like those of **birds**. The ornithischians include many kinds of plant-eating dinosaurs, such as **stegosaurs**, **ankylosaurs** and **ornithopods**.

Ornitholestes *noun*

Ornitholestes was a small **dinosaur** from the **Jurassic Period**. It belonged to the **coelurosaur** group. Ornitholestes was about two metres long and ran well on its long hind legs. It fed on small animals.

Ornithomimus *noun*

Ornithomimus was a **dinosaur** from the **Cretaceous Period**. It was a little like an ostrich in shape and grew to about four metres long. *Ornithomimus* had a horny beak, like a bird's, and probably ate leaves, fruit and small animals. Its strong back legs allowed *Ornithomimus* to chase after its animal prey, catching them with its hands. Fossils of *Ornithomimus* have been found in North America.

ornithomimosaur *noun*

The ornithomimosaurs are a group of **dinosaurs** which lived in the late **Jurassic** and **Cretaceous Periods**. They belonged to the **theropod** group. The ornithomimosaurs were fast-running dinosaurs. They had long, ostrich-like hind legs and large eyes. They also lacked teeth, but had hard, horny jaws. Ornithomimosaurs were about three or four metres long. They included ***Ornithomimus***, ***Oviraptor***, ***Struthiomimus*** and ***Gallimimus***.

ornithopod *noun*

The ornithopods, or bird-footed **dinosaurs**, are a group of dinosaurs which lived in the **Jurassic** and **Cretaceous Periods**. About 70 different species of ornithopod have been discovered. They include ***Anatosaurus***, ***Dryosaurus***, ***Fabrosaurus*** and ***Iguanodon***. The ornithopods were all plant-eaters, or **herbivores**. They were the only **ornithischians** which could walk or run on their hind legs.

Ordovician Period *noun*

The Ordovician Period was a time in **geological history**. The Ordovician Period lasted from about 505 million years ago to about 438 million years ago. Most life on Earth during the Ordovician Period was found in the sea. **Trilobites** and **brachiopods** were common. There were also colonies of **graptolites**, and the first corals appeared. Early **agnathans** also lived in the Ordovician Period.

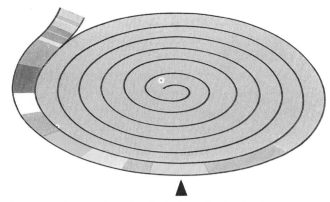

The arrow shows where the Ordovician Period lies in relation to the geological history of the Earth.

1. eurypterid
2. crinoid
3. nautiloid
4. coral
5. brachiopod
6. burrowing worms
7. trilobite

Ornithosuchus *noun*
Ornithosuchus was a **reptile** which lived in the **Triassic Period**. It belonged to the **thecodont** group. *Ornithosuchus* was about four metres long and fed on other animals. Unlike most true **dinosaurs**, *Ornithosuchus* probably walked on all fours most of the time.

Orthoceras *noun*
Orthoceras was a kind of **mollusc** called a **nautiloid**. *Orthoceras* lived from the **Ordovician Period** until the **Triassic Period**. *Orthoceras* reached several metres in length. It swam in the open ocean and moved along by squirting out jets of water. Unlike most nautiloids, *Orthoceras* had a straight shell shaped like a cone.

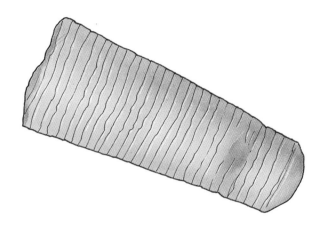

Osmunda *noun*
Osmunda is a kind of **fern**. It is also known as the royal fern. There are about 10 species of *Osmunda* alive today. The earliest fossils of *Osmunda* date from the **Cretaceous Period**. Early kinds probably lived near water in warm or tropical areas.

osteichthian *noun*
An osteichthian is one of a **class** of **fish**. The osteichthians are the bony fish. There are about 25,000 species of osteichthian alive today. Most belong to the ray-finned group, or **actinopterygians**. The osteichthian evolved in the **Devonian Period**. *Lepidotus* and the **coclacanth** are examples of osteichthians.

Othnielia *noun*
Othnielia was an **ornithopod dinosaur**. It lived during the upper **Jurassic Period**, and was very similar in appearance to *Hypsilophodon*.

Ouranosaurus *noun*
Ouranosaurus was a **dinosaur** which lived in the **Cretaceous Period**, in Africa. It belonged to the **ornithopod** group. *Ouranosaurus* looked a little like *Iguanodon*, but was slightly smaller, measuring about seven metres in length. *Ouranosaurus* had a sail along its back, which was supported by spiny bones. It probably used this to cool down in hot weather and to warm itself in the Sun when it was cold.

oviparous *adjective*
Oviparous describes an animal that lays eggs. Many animals are oviparous, including most **invertebrates**. Of the **vertebrates**, most fish, amphibians, reptiles and birds are oviparous. The **dinosaurs** were also oviparous since all their young hatched from eggs. The only mammals that lay eggs are the **monotremes**.

Oviraptor *noun*
Oviraptor was a small **dinosaur** which lived in the **Cretaceous Period**. It belonged to the **coelurosaur** group. *Oviraptor* had a wide, bony beak, rather like that of a large bird. It also had a small horn on its snout. It may have fed on the eggs of other dinosaurs.

Oxyaena *noun*
Oxyaena was a **mammal** which lived in the **Paleocene** and **Eocene Epochs**. It was about the size of a dog, and had long **canine** teeth for grasping and killing its prey. *Oxyaena* belonged to a group of early mammals called the **creodonts**. Fossils of *Oxyaena* have been found in North America and in Europe.

oxygen *noun*
Oxygen is a chemical element. It is a colourless gas which is found in the atmosphere. Oxygen is the most common element in the Earth's crust. Nearly all living things need oxygen to survive. Green plants give out oxygen in the process called photosynthesis.

Oxynoticeras *noun*
Oxynoticeras was a **ammonite** which lived in the **Jurassic Period**. Its shell was divided into compartments that were filled with gas. The shape of its shell indicates that it was probably a fast swimmer.

pachycephalosaur *noun*
The pachycephalosaurs were a group of **dinosaurs**. They lived in the **Cretaceous Period**, mainly in North America and Asia. They had a heavy, broad skull. ***Stegoceras*** is an example of a pachycephalosaur.

Pakicetus *noun*
Pakicetus is a kind of whale. It is one of the earliest types of whale known, and lived in the **Eocene Epoch**. A few fossilized remains of *Pakicetus* were found in Pakistan, in 1981. It is not possible to tell from these how large the animal was. Fossils show that it had sharp teeth and may have had a rather dog-like head.

Palaeocastor *noun*
Palaeocastor is a kind of extinct beaver. It lived in the **Oligocene** and **Miocene Epochs** in North America and Asia. It lived rather like a prairie dog, in burrows.

Palaeoloxodon *noun*
Palaeoloxodon was a kind of elephant. It lived in the middle of the **Pleistocene Epoch**. *Palaeoloxodon* had straight tusks.

palaeothere *noun*
The palaeotheres were a group of hoofed **mammals** which lived in Europe during the **Eocene** and **Oligocene Epochs**. They were related to horses, but had a snout.

Paleocene Epoch ► page 107

Paleogene *noun*
The Paleogene is a division of **geological history**. It is the earliest part of the **Tertiary Period**, lasting from 65 until 26 million years ago. The Paleogene includes the **Paleocene**, **Eocene** and **Oligocene Epochs**.

Paleolithic *adjective*
Paleolithic describes an archaeological **period**. It lasted from about 3.5 million until about 10,000 years ago. The Paleolithic period is also called the Stone Age. Most **cave art** dates from the Paleolithic period.

paleontologist *noun*
A paleontologist is a scientist who studies **fossils**. Some paleontologists collect and describe fossils. Others use fossils to help make a picture or model of extinct species, and reconstruct ancient environments.

paleontology ► page 108

Paleozoic Era *noun*
The Paleozoic Era is one of the main divisions of **geological history**. It lasted from about 590 until about 248 million years ago.

Pangaea *noun*
Pangaea was a large mass of land, called a **super-continent**. It formed about 240 million years ago, in the **Triassic Period**. Pangaea gradually split up, eventually forming the **continents** we know today.

Panthalassa *noun*
Panthalassa is the name of the ocean which surrounded **Pangaea**. It existed between about 240 and 150 million years ago.

pantotheria *noun*
The pantotheria were a group of **mammals** which lived in the **Jurassic Period**. The pantotheria were small, shrew-like **insectivores**. They gave birth to live young. Both the **marsupials** and the **placental mammals** developed from the pantotheria.

Paramys *noun*
Paramys was a small **mammal** which lived in the **Paleocene** and **Eocene Epochs**, in North America and Europe. It was about half a metre long, with a long tail like a squirrel's. *Paramys* was one of the first **rodents**. Like today's rodents, it had large incisor teeth which it used for gnawing.

Parasaurolophus *noun*
Parasaurolophus was a duck-billed dinosaur, or **hadrosaur**. It lived in the **Cretaceous Period** in North America. *Parasaurolophus* grew to about 10 metres long, and had a long, powerful tail. Its strangest feature was the long, backward-curving, bony crest on its head. This crest contained hollow tubes which joined with the nose. It may have been used to make loud, booming noises.

pelvis *noun*
The pelvis is the **hip** girdle in a **vertebrate** animal. It is made of three bones. These are the **ilium**, the **ischium** and the **pubis**. In the two groups of **dinosaurs**, the bird-hipped and the lizard-hipped, the bones of the pelvis are arranged differently.

Paleocene Epoch   *noun*

The Paleocene Epoch was a time in **geological history**. The Paleocene Epoch lasted from about 65 million years ago to about 55 million years ago. During the Paleocene Epoch, Europe and North America were still joined together. The first carnivorous mammals appeared. These mammals were called creodonts. Early rodents lived during the Paleocene Epoch. These rodents had long incisors that were used for gnawing.

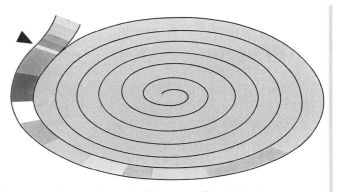

The arrow shows where the Paleocene Epoch lies in relation to the geological history of the Earth.

1. *Plesiadapis*
2. *Phenacodus*
3. *Oxyaena*
4. *Paramys*
5. *Taeniolabis*

paleontology   *noun*

Paleontology is the study of **fossils**. Scientists who study fossils are called paleontologists. Some paleontologists find fossils by digging them carefully out of **rock**. Other paleontologists study the fossils in a laboratory. A lot of information can be learned from fossil remains, about the lives of extinct animals and plants. Every year, new discoveries are made, though there are still many unsolved fossil mysteries.

Many fossil remains have been found in caves underground.

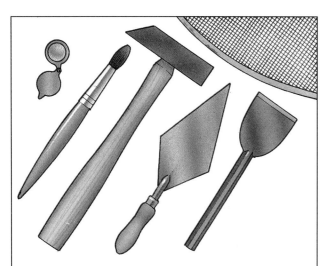

A paleontologist's field tools may include a hand lens, a brush, a geological hammer, a trowel, a wide chisel and a sieve.

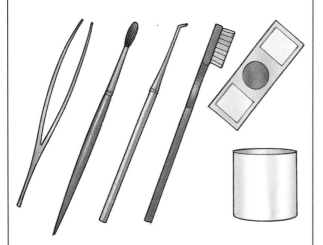

Laboratory tools may include tweezers, a fine brush, a probe, a toothbrush, a microscope slide and a specimen box.

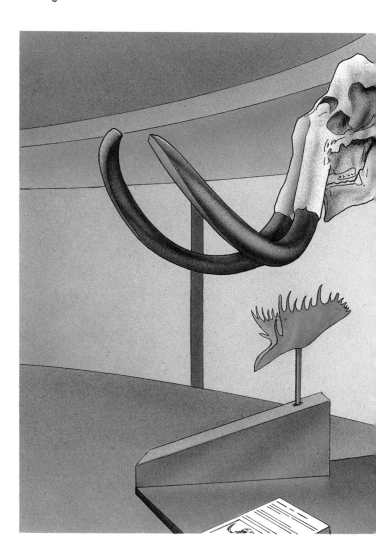

Discoveries are sometimes made in rock close to the Earth's surface.

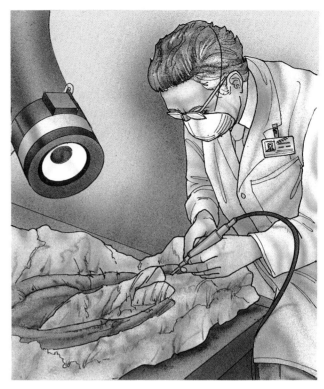

Fossils are carefully cleaned in the laboratory.

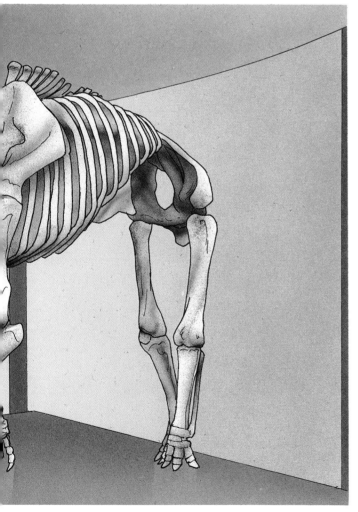

Bones may be reconstructed to show what a whole skeleton looked like.

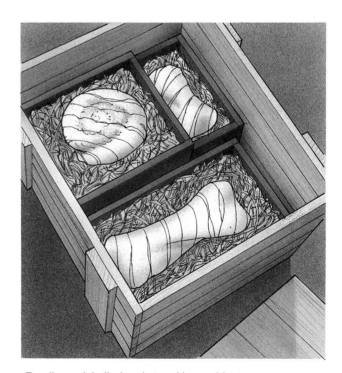

Fossils are labelled and stored in a cabinet.

pelycosaur   *noun*
A pelycosaur was one of a group of
synapsid reptiles. Many pelycosaurs had
large, sail-like fins on their back. The
pelycosaurs lived in the **Carboniferous** and
Permian Periods. *Edaphosaurus* and
Dimetrodon are examples of pelycosaurs.

Pennsylvanian Epoch   *noun*
The Pennsylvanian Epoch was a time in
geological history. The Pennsylvanian
Epoch is the later part of the **Carboniferous
Period**. In Europe, the Pennsylvanian Epoch
is usually known as the Upper Carboniferous
Period.

Pentaceratops   *noun*
Pentaceratops was a **dinosaur** which lived
in the **Cretaceous Period**, in North America.
It belonged to the **ceratopsid** group.
Pentaceratops had a heavy body with a
large frill covering its neck. Like
Triceratops, it had three long horns on its
head. *Pentaceratops* used its horns to
defend itself against carnivorous dinosaurs.
It also had a spike sticking out from each
cheek.

period   *noun*
A period is one of the main divisions of
geological history. Each **era** is divided into
two or more periods. The oldest period is the
Azoic, and the most recent is the
Quaternary. Scientists divide periods into
epochs. The length of each period varies,
depending on the changes to life shown by
fossils.

permafrost   *noun*
Permafrost is ground which is permanently
frozen. Permafrost is found in regions which
are very cold, such as in the Arctic. The
preserved remains of **mammoths** have
occasionally been found in permafrost.

Permian Period ► page 111

petrification   *noun*
Petrification, or petrifaction, is a form of
fossilization. In this process, the hard parts
of an animal are turned to stone. This
happens when minerals from the soil
gradually replace the animal's skeleton. The
most common minerals involved are **calcite**,
silica and mixtures of iron.
petrify   *verb*

petrified forest   *noun*
A petrified forest is a wood which has been
turned into **fossils**. The wood in the trees is
gradually replaced by **silica** from water rich
in mineral salts. The most famous example
is in the Petrified Forest National Park in
Arizona, United States of America.

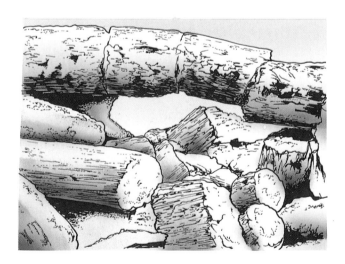

Petrolacosaurus   *noun*
Petrolacosaurus was a lizard-like **reptile**
which lived in the **Carboniferous Period**.
It belonged to the **diapsid** group. Lizards,
dinosaurs, pterosaurs and crocodiles are all
thought to have evolved from early reptiles
such as *Petrolacosaurus*.

Permian Period   *noun*

The Permian Period was a time in **geological history**. The Permian Period lasted from about 286 million years ago to about 248 million years ago. Many ancient species became extinct during the Permian Period, including **trilobites**. Many new reptiles appeared, including mammal-like reptiles such as ***Moschops***. Some amphibians alive during the Permian Period developed some reptile-like features.

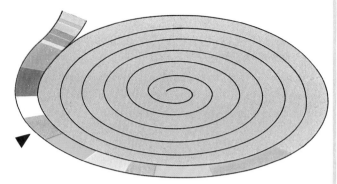

The arrow shows where the Permian Period lies in relation to the geological history of the Earth.

1. *Dimetrodon*
2. *Moschops*
3: *Weigeltisaurus*
4. *Diplocaulus*
5. *Youngina*

111

Phanerozoic Eon   *noun*

The Phanerozoic Eon is one of the main divisions of **geological history**. It began about 590 million years ago and includes the present day. It is the most recent **eon**. All the periods from the **Cambrian** to the present day are part of the **Phanerozoic Eon**.

Phenacodus   *noun*

Phenacodus was a mammal which lived in the **Paleocene** and **Eocene Epochs**. It belonged to the **condylarth** group. *Phenacodus* was probably an early form of **ungulate**. It was about 1.5 metres long and had a long tail. Horses may have developed from *Phenacodus*. Unlike horses, however, *Phenacodus* had five fingers and five toes, not hooves.

Phorusrhacus   *noun*

Phorusrhacus was a giant, flightless bird. It lived in the **Miocene Epoch**, in South America. *Phorusrhacus* was shaped a little like an emu, with a long neck and long legs. It was about 1.5 metres tall. But *Phorusrhacus* had a beak like that of a huge eagle, with a strongly hooked tip. *Phorusrhacus* probably developed apart from the similar ***Diatryma***. If it did, this made a good example of **convergent evolution**.

Phyllodus   *noun*

Phyllodus was a bony fish which lived in the **Eocene Epoch**, in North America and Europe. It probably fed on small marine animals, such as molluscs.

phylum (plural **phyla**)   *noun*

A phylum is a rank in the classification of animals. It is the main category between kingdom and **class**. There are about 33 phyla in the animal kingdom. The phyla differ widely in size, some including many thousands of species, and others very few. The animals in one phylum share the same basic body-plan. **Molluscs**, roundworms, **arthropods** and **chordates** are all examples of animal phyla.

Piatnitzkysaurus   *noun*

Piatnitzkysaurus was a **carnosaur** which lived in the **Jurassic Period** in Argentina, South America. It was similar to ***Allosaurus***. *Piatnitzkysaurus* grew to about four metres long, and walked and ran on its powerful hind legs. It had a large head with long, pointed teeth.

Pinacosaurus   *noun*

Pinacosaurus was a **dinosaur** which lived in the **Cretaceous Period**. It belonged to the **ankylosaur** group. *Pinacosaurus* looked similar to ***Ankylosaurus***, but was smaller, at around five metres long. Its head was protected with bony plates and it had a beak. Fossils of *Pinacosaurus* have been discovered in Mongolia.

piscivore   *noun*

A piscivore is an animal which feeds on fish. There were many piscivores amongst prehistoric animals. These included the **plesiosaurs** and the **ichthyosaurs**.

placental mammal   *noun*

A placental mammal is a member of one of the main groups of **mammals**. In this group, the young develop inside the mother's body and are fed by a special organ, the placenta. The other groups of mammals are the **marsupials** and the **monotremes**. Most living and extinct mammals are placental. Placental mammals first appeared in the late **Cretaceous Period**. The earliest placental mammals included the **condylarths**.

placoderm   *noun*
A placoderm was an early form of **fish** which lived during the **Devonian Period**. The body of placoderms was protected by an armour of heavy, bony plates. The placoderms became extinct in the early **Carboniferous Period**.

placodont   *noun*
A placodont was one of a **family** of **reptiles** which lived in the **Triassic Period**. Some placodonts were shaped rather like turtles, others resembled the **notosaurs**. Many placodonts fed on shellfish.

plant ▶ page 114

plate tectonics   *plural noun*
Plate tectonics is the study of movements in the Earth's crust. The crust is divided into a number of plates which move very gradually over long periods of time and press against each other. The **super-continents** moved by plate tectonics to form the **continents** we know today.

Plateosaurus   *noun*
Plateosaurus was a large **dinosaur** which lived in the **Triassic Period**. It belonged to the **prosauropod** group, and grew to about eight metres long. Many well-preserved fossils of *Plateosaurus* have been discovered, mostly in Europe. *Plateosaurus* had a long neck and tail. It also had large hands with long claws, but like its relatives it was probably a **herbivore**.

Platybelodon   *noun*
Platybelodon was an ancestor of the elephant. It lived in the **Miocene Epoch**, in Asia and North America. *Platybelodon* had a flat, trunk-like nose and short tusks in its upper jaw. Its lower jaw had two flat tusks which it used like a shovel to scrape up water plants to eat.

Pleistocene Epoch ▶ page 116

Plesiadapis   *noun*
Plesiadapis was a small **mammal**. It was one of the first primates. *Plesiadapis* lived in the **Paleocene** and early **Eocene Epochs**. It looked like a squirrel, and possibly lived in the trees.

plesiosaur   *noun*
A plesiosaur was an **aquatic reptile**. The plesiosaurs lived in the **Jurassic Period**. They included *Cryptoclidus*, *Elasmosaurus* and *Plesiosaurus*. The largest were about 15 metres long.

Plesiosaurus   *noun*
Plesiosaurus was an **aquatic reptile** which lived in the **Jurassic Period**. It was about five metres long and its body shape was well adapted to swimming in water. *Plesiosaurus* had paddle-like limbs and a long neck. Its jaws had sharp teeth and it fed on fish. Fossils of *Plesiosaurus* were first discovered in England in the early 1800s.

plant   *noun*

A plant is a living organism that makes its food from inorganic matter. Most plants, but not all, have some green parts because they contain a substance called chlorophyll. Plants called **algae** were the first living things in the world. They lived in the sea. Algae released oxygen into the atmosphere and this changed the balance of gases around the Earth. The first plants to live on the land appeared during the **Silurian Period**.

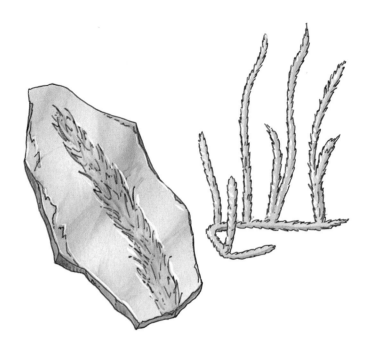

Baragwanatha was a low-growing plant that grew in lowland areas. It first appeared in the late Silurian Period.

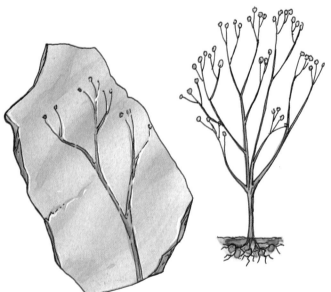

Cooksonia lived during the late Silurian and Devonian Periods. It is the earliest known land plant. It grew about six centimetres tall.

Glossopteris was a tree-sized seedfern. Its leaves were similar in shape to banana leaves. It lived during the Permian Period.

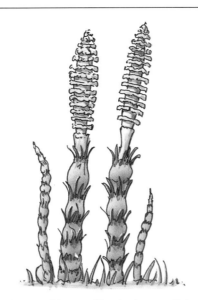

The modern horsetail is very like the horsetail that lived from the Carboniferous to Cretaceous Periods. Horsetails spread by sending out stems underground.

Osmunda is a kind of fern that still exists today. It grows near water in warm regions. Fossils of *Osmunda* have been found dating from the Cretaceous Period.

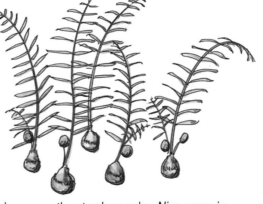

Nipa is also known as the stemless palm. *Nipa* grows in mangrove swamps in South-east Asia. Fossils of *Nipa* have been found dating from the Cretaceous Period.

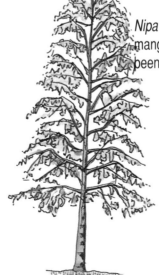

The *Betula*, or birch tree, first appeared in the Miocene Epoch.

Ficus is a fig tree. Fossilized fruits of the fig tree have been found dating back to the Eocene Epoch.

Pleistocene Epoch *noun*

The Pleistocene Epoch was a time in **geological history**. It lasted from about two million years ago to about 10,000 years ago. Ice covered large areas of the Earth in many **glaciations** during the Pleistocene Epoch. Many animals, such as the woolly mammoth, developed thick fur as protection against the freezing temperatures. Early **hominids** lived during the Pleistocene Epoch, and *Homo sapiens* first appeared about 100,000 years ago, in Africa.

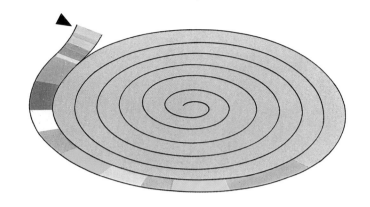

The arrow shows where the Pleistocene Epoch lies in relation to the geological history of the Earth.

1. *Sivatherium*
2. *Deinotherium*
3. *Smilodon*
4. *Megaloceros*
5. *Homo sapiens*
6. *Diprotodon*
7. *Glypton*
8. *hyena*

Pliocene Epoch *noun*

The Pliocene Epoch was a time in **geological history**. The Pliocene Epoch lasted from about 5 million years ago to about 2 million years ago. Large herbivorous mammals such as mammoths, bisons and rhinoceroses lived during the Pliocene Epoch. The first known **hominids** date from about 4 or 5 million years ago. These early hominids walked upright, and had a larger brain than their ape-like ancestors.

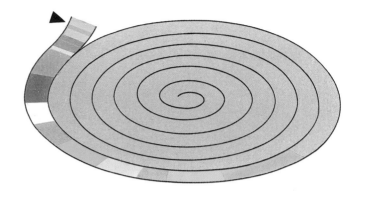

The arrow shows where the Pliocene Epoch lies in relation to the geological history of the Earth.

1. *Megatherium*
2. *Dicerorhinus*
3. *Thylacosmilus*
4. *Australopithecus*
5. *Argyrolagus*
6. mammoth
7. bison
8. *Hipparion*

Pleurosaurus *noun*
Pleurosaurus was a small **aquatic reptile** which lived in the **Jurassic** and **Cretaceous Periods**. Its short limbs could still be used for walking as well as swimming, so it probably led an **amphibious** life. *Pleurosaurus* may be related to the **tuataras**.

Pliocene Epoch ▶ page 118

Pliohippus *noun*
Pliohippus was a horse which appeared in the **Pliocene Epoch**, in North America. It became extinct about five million years ago. *Pliohippus* was the first one-toed horse, with a hoof-like toe on each foot.

Pliosaurus *noun*
Pliosaurus was an **aquatic reptile** which lived in the **Jurassic Period**. It belonged to the **plesiosaur** group. *Pliosaurus* was about 12 metres in length, with a long head. It had short, broad teeth and probably fed mainly on molluscs.

Precambrian Period ▶ page 122

predator *noun*
A predator is an animal which hunts and feeds on other animals. Predators have highly efficient bodies for catching their prey. These include strong jaws with sharp teeth for biting and ripping flesh, high-speed running or flight, and well-developed claws or talons.
predatory *adjective*

prehistory *noun*
Prehistory is the time before history began to be recorded. History was first recorded about 40,000 years ago. The animals that lived during prehistory are called prehistoric animals. The **dinosaurs** are the most famous of these. Other examples are **ammonites**, **trilobites** and **mammoths**. The oldest prehistoric animals lived in the sea about 600 million years ago.
prehistoric *adjective*

Priscoan Eon ▶ **Azoic Eon**

Probelesodon *noun*
Probelesodon was a mammal-like **reptile** which lived in the **Triassic Period**, in South America. It was a member of the **cynodont** group. *Probelesodon* was a **carnivore** and looked like a dog with a long snout. It was probably **warm-blooded** and covered in hair.

Procolophon *noun*
Procolophon was a **reptile** which lived in the **Triassic Period**. It belonged to the **anapsid** group. *Procolophon* was like a lizard in shape and about 30 centimetres long. It had large eyes and a triangular head. *Procolophon* was probably a **herbivore**.

Proconsul *noun*
Proconsul was one of the first of the **hominoids**. Scientists think it was a true ape. *Proconsul* lived in the **Miocene Epoch**, and its fossils have been found in East Africa. It was about one metre in height and probably climbed trees.

Procoptodon *noun*
Procoptodon was a giant kangaroo. It lived in the **Pleistocene Epoch** in Australia. *Procoptodon* reached a height of about three metres.

Proganochelys *noun*
Proganochelys was a kind of turtle. It lived in the **Triassic Period**, and its fossils have been found in Asia and Europe. *Proganochelys* grew to about one metre long. Like living turtles, it had a bony shell, large eyes and horny jaws. *Proganochelys* fed on plants. It was **amphibious**.

progymnosperm *noun*
A progymnosperm was a **plant** which lived in the **Devonian Period**. The progymnosperm group includes species about the size of tree ferns, but also larger trees, up to about 10 metres tall. They fall between the **pteridophytes** and **gymnosperms**. The progymnosperms probably developed into the gymnosperms. They were some of the first trees on Earth.

prosauropod *noun*
A prosauropod was one of a group of medium-sized and large **dinosaurs**. The prosauropods lived in the **Triassic** and **Jurassic Periods**. They had a heavy body, with a long neck and tail. Some walked on two legs, some on four. Examples of prosauropods are ***Anchisaurus***, ***Lufengosaurus*** and ***Plateosaurus***.

Proterozoic Eon *noun*
The Proterozoic Eon was a time in **geological history**. It lasted from about 2,500 million to about 590 million years ago. The Proterozoic Eon is the later part of the **Precambrian Era**. Life first appeared in the sea during the Proterozoic Eon.

protist *noun*
A protist is a tiny living thing, or **organism**. Protists form a kingdom of their own, the *Protista*. About 120,000 species have been named, about half of which are fossil kinds. Most protists are too small to be seen without a microscope. They are found in land and water all over the world. Scientists think that all animals, plants and fungi evolved from protists.

Protoceratops *noun*
Protoceratops was a horned **dinosaur** which lived in the **Cretaceous Period**, in Asia. It was about two metres long and had short legs. Its most obvious feature was its large, bony frill arching back over its neck. *Protoceratops* browsed on plants and used its powerful beak to shear off stems. Whole nests of **fossilized** *Protoceratops* eggs have been discovered, together with adult skeletons.

protoceratopsid *noun*
A protoceratopsid was a member of one of the families of horned dinosaurs, or **ceratopsians**. The protoceratopsids had short legs and walked on all fours. They were **herbivores** and belonged to the lizard-hipped group of dinosaurs, or **saurischians**.

Precambrian Period *noun*

The Precambrian Period was a time in **geological history**. The Precambrian Period lasted from about 4,600 million years ago to about 590 million years ago. Many ancient rocks date from the Precambrian Period. The first forms of life evolved during this time. **Algae** lived in the sea, and jellyfish, worms and other **invertebrates** developed.

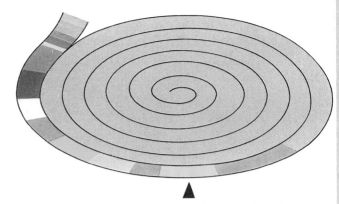

The arrow shows where the Precambrian Period lies in relation to the geological history of the Earth.

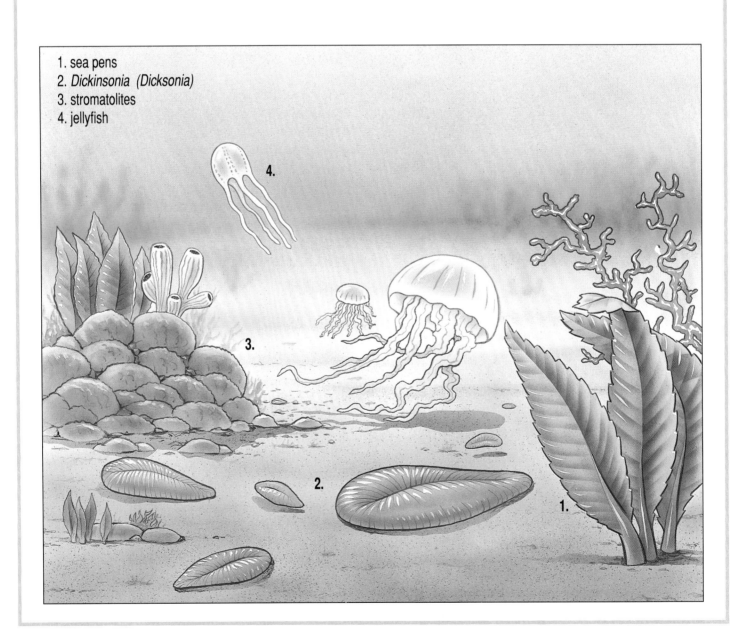

1. sea pens
2. *Dickinsonia (Dicksonia)*
3. stromatolites
4. jellyfish

Protorosaurus *noun*
Protorosaurus was a **diapsid reptile** from the **Permian Period**. It was about 1.2 metres in length, and looked rather like a large lizard. *Protorosaurus* had long back legs and it could probably stand up on these when necessary. It fed on small animals such as insects.

Protosuchus *noun*
Protosuchus was a **crocodilian**. It lived in the **Jurassic Period**. *Protosuchus* grew to a length of about one metre. It had a shorter snout than modern crocodiles and spent less time in the water. Protosuchus probably ate small mammals and other land animals as well as fish.

prototheria *plural noun*
The prototheria are one of the two main groups of **mammals**. They are the egg-laying mammals. The prototheria evolved from mammal-like **reptiles** in the **Jurassic Period**. The only prototheria alive today are the **monotremes**. The other mammal group is the **theria**.

protozoan ► **protist**

Psittacosaurus *noun*
Psittacosaurus was a **reptile** which lived in the **Cretaceous Period**. It belonged to the horned dinosaur group, or **ceratopsians**. *Psittacosaurus* was about two metres long and walked on its hind legs. It had a large, heavy head with a horny beak and frill.

Pteranodon *noun*
Pteranodon was the best known of the flying reptiles, or **pterosaurs**. It lived in the **Cretaceous Period**, and its fossils have been found in North America. *Pteranodon* had bat-like wings made of stretched skin, and these were up to about seven metres across. It probably had a slow, flapping and gliding flight. *Pteranodon* had a long beak with a bony projection sticking out backwards from its head. This may have balanced the weight of the beak in flight.

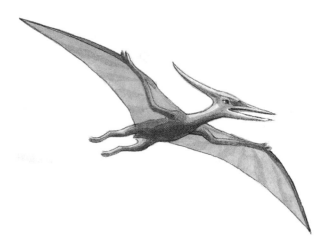

Pteraspis *noun*
Pteraspis was a jawless **fish** which lived in the **Devonian Period**. It grew to about 25 centimetres long and its head was protected by large, bony plates. Fossils of *Pteraspis* have been found in Asia, Europe and North America.

pteridophyte *noun*
A pteridophyte is a member of the group of **plants** that includes **ferns**, **club mosses** and **horsetails**. Pteridophytes are also known as fern plants. There are many examples of fossil pteridophytes, as they were very common during past times. Pteridophytes do not produce flowers and seeds, unlike the other major group of plants, the **angiosperms**. Instead they reproduce by sending out spores. Pteridophytes were very common in the **Carboniferous Period**.

Pterodactylus *noun*
Pterodactylus was a **flying reptile** which lived in the **Jurassic Period**. It belonged to the **pterosaur** group. *Pterodactylus* had a long, horny beak and pointed, leathery wings. It probably fed mainly on fish. It was much smaller than *Pteranodon*, reaching about 30 centimetres in length, and flew well, with an active, flapping flight.

pterosaur *noun*
A pterosaur was a member of a group of **flying reptiles**. The pterosaurs lived mainly in the **Jurassic Period**. Some, like *Pterodactylus*, were quite small. Others, such as *Pteranodon* and *Quetzalcoatlus*, were much larger than the biggest flying birds. Pterosaurs had very light, hollow bones and usually had sharp teeth. They fed mainly on fish. Their wings were made of skin stretched tightly between the body and the fourth finger of each hand.

Pterygotus *noun*
Pterygotus was a water scorpion, or **eurypterid**. It lived in the **Devonian Period**. Its back pair of legs were shaped like paddles, for swimming. *Pterygotus* was the largest **arthropod** of all time, at nearly two metres long.

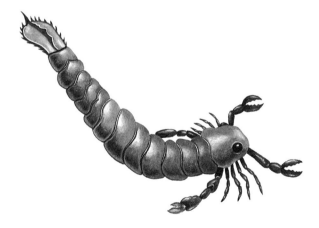

pubis *noun*
The pubis is a **bone**. It is one of the three bones making up the **hip** of a **vertebrate** animal. The other bones of the hip are the **ilium** and **ischium**.

Purgatorius *noun*
Purgatorius was a small **mammal**. It was one of the earliest of the primates, and lived in the **Cretaceous Period** and early **Tertiary Period**. *Purgatorius* was about 25 centimetres long and looked rather like a mouse lemur. It was **nocturnal** and probably ate insects, leaves and fruit.

Pyrotherium *noun*
Pyrotherium was a **mammal** which lived in South America in the **Oligocene Epoch**. It was shaped like a **hippopotamus** and grew to about four metres long. *Pyrotherium* had a short, flexible snout and six short tusks. It was a **herbivore** and fed on plants.

Quetzalcoatlus   *noun*
Quetzalcoatlus was a flying reptile, or **pterosaur**. It lived in the **Cretaceous Period**. *Quetzalcoatlus* was the largest flying animal ever to have lived. Its wingspan was at least 11 metres. Fossils of *Quetzalcoatlus* have been found in Texas.

quadruped   *noun*
A quadruped is an animal which moves on four legs. Many mammals walk, run or jump on all fours. Examples of quadrupeds include mice, pigs, horses and elephants. Some mammals, such as the apes, can walk on two legs. They are known as **bipedal**.
quadrupedal   *adjective*

quagga   *noun*
A quagga was a member of the horse family. It looked rather like a zebra, but had stripes only at the front of its body. The quagga lived in South Africa. It became extinct in the 1880s.

Quaternary Period   *noun*
The Quaternary Period is a time in **geological history**. The Quaternary Period is the most recent of all the geological periods. It began about 2 million years ago, and continues to the present day. During the Quaternary Period, **humans** first appeared on the Earth.

Quercus   *noun*
Quercus is a genus of tree. It is also known as the oak. The earliest oaks appeared in the **Eocene Epoch**. Many fossilized parts of *Quercus* have been identified, including wood, leaves and pollen.

quern   *noun*
A quern is a kind of mill for grinding grain. It consists of two circular stones. The grain is placed between the stones and is ground as the upper stone is rotated. Querns were first used during the **Iron Age**.

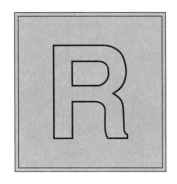

radioactivity *noun*
Radioactivity is the process by which atoms give off radiation. Some elements, such as uranium and radium, have natural radioactivity. Radioactivity is measured using a Geiger counter. **Rocks** and **fossils** can be dated by measuring their radioactivity.

Ramapithecus *noun*
Ramapithecus was a **mammal** which lived in the **Miocene** and **Pliocene Epochs**, about 15 million years ago. Like *Proconsul*, it belonged to the **hominoid** group of primates. *Ramapithecus* was about 1.2 metres tall, and its fossils have been found in Africa and Asia.

Rastrites *noun*
Rastrites was an **invertebrate** belonging to the **graptolite** group. Its fossils are found in **shales**, from many parts of the world. *Rastrites* lived during the **Silurian Period**. *Rastrites* lived in colonies in the open sea. The fossils show as delicate, feathery curves, about four centimetres long.

ray-finned fish ► **actinopterygian**

reconstruction *noun*
Reconstruction describes how an extinct animal is re-formed from its **fossils**. Most fossils are made up of a collection of bones rather than the whole animal. So **paleontologists** have to reconstruct the shape of the extinct creature using their knowledge of living animals.
reconstruct *verb*

red alga (plural **algae**) *noun*
A red alga is one of a group of simple plants, or **algae**. Red algae are **protists**. They mostly live in the sea, and are found in shallow and deep waters. Many red algae produce hard substances such as **calcite**. Such red algae were common in the **Paleozoic** and **Mesozoic Eras**. Coralline algae also belong to this group. They first appeared during the **Cambrian Period**.

redwood ► **Sequoia**

relative dating *noun*
Relative dating is a method of working out the date of **geological** finds. In relative dating, the age of **rocks** or **fossils** is worked out compared, or relative, to other rocks or fossils found nearby. **Index fossils** are used in relative dating. The other kind of dating is **absolute dating**.

resin ► **amber**

reptile *noun*
A reptile is a kind of **vertebrate** animal. There are about 6,500 species of reptile. They include snakes, lizards, turtles and crocodiles, as well as the extinct **dinosaurs**. Reptiles are cold-blooded. Most species live on land and are **carnivorous**. Most reptiles have a tough, waterproof skin covered in scales. Apart from snakes, reptiles have four legs, and usually a long tail. Like birds, reptiles lay eggs, but the eggs of reptiles are large and leathery.

reptile-hipped dinosaur ► **saurischian**

Rhamphorhynchus *noun*
Rhamphorhynchus was one of the earliest of the flying reptiles, or **pterosaurs**. It lived in the **Jurassic Period** in Africa and Europe. It was about 20 centimetres long and unlike the later pterosaurs, it had a long tail, with a kite-like sail at the tip, for steering.

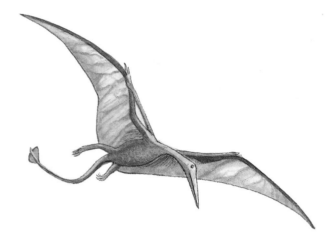

rhinoceros *noun*
A rhinoceros is a large, hoofed **mammal**. There are five living species of rhinoceros, in Africa and South-east Asia. They have very tough skin and short, thick legs with hoofed feet. The head has one or two long, curved horns. The horn of a rhinoceros is not made of bone, but of compressed hair. Rhinoceroses live in grassland habitats. They are **herbivores**, feeding on grass and twigs. Rhinoceroses were common in the **Tertiary Period**. The woolly rhinoceros, or *Coelodonta*, survived until about 15,000 years ago.

rhynchosaur *noun*
A rhynchosaur is a member of a group of extinct **reptiles**. The rhynchosaurs belonged to the **diapsid** class and were common in the **Triassic Period**. Rhynchosaurs were **herbivores**. They had a large, heavy body. *Hyperodapedon* is an example of a rhynchosaur.

Rhynia *noun*
Rhynia was a **plant** belonging to the **pteridophyte** group. It was one of the earliest plants in this group, and lived in the **Silurian** and **Devonian Periods**. *Rhynia* was about 50 centimetres high and had branching stems with simple spores.

rock ► page 128

rodent *noun*
A rodent is a member of an **order** of small **mammals**. Rodents have sharp **incisor** teeth which they use for gnawing their food. There are about 1,700 species of living rodent, including mice, squirrels and beavers. *Paramys* was one of the first rodents to evolve.

roofed lizard ► **stegosaur**

royal fern ► **Osmunda**

127

rock *noun*

Rock is a hard mineral deposit. Rock is made up of different combinations of minerals. The Earth's crust is made of rocks about 70 kilometres deep. The main types of rocks are igneous, metamorphic and sedimentary rocks. They are named after the way they were formed. The rocks in the Earth's crust have been forming for over 4,000 million years. **Fossils** are often found in sedimentary rock.

In the Grand Canyon, Arizona, USA, layers of sedimentary rocks have built up over about 700 million years. Fossils are found in most of the layers of rock.

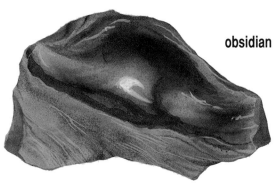

obsidian

Igneous rocks are formed from molten material inside the Earth. Obsidian is a glass-like igneous rock formed from cooled lava. Its sharp edges made it useful as an early cutting tool.

marble

Metamorphic rock is rock that has been changed by high pressure and hardened by heating.

128

Sedimentary rock is formed by layers of sediment.
Small pieces of rock and shells build up and
become cemented together by pressure.
Many fossils are found in sedimentary rock.

limestone

Stegosaurus from the
Jurassic Period

Dimetrodon from the
Permian Period

Xenacanthus from the
Carboniferous Period

Paradoxides from the
Cambrian Period

Collenia, an algae from the
Precambrian Period

Thick layers of vegetation die and start to rot.

The compacted vegetation forms peat.
Some plant roots and seed cases can be
seen in peat.

Lignite is a brown, crumbly substance made
when peat is compressed.

The lignite turns into black, dusty coal.

Anthracite is harder than ordinary coal,
and gives out more heat.

Coal began to form during the Carboniferous Period.
It formed from plant material that was compressed over
millions of years.

sabre-toothed cat ▶ **machairodont**

sail *noun*
A sail is a large, fan-like fin on the back of some kinds of **dinosaur**. Reptiles of the **pelycosaur** group, such as *Dimetrodon* and *Edaphosaurus*, probably used their sails to absorb heat from the Sun, and perhaps also to cool down in hot weather.

sail-backed reptile ▶ **pelycosaur**

salamander *noun*
A salamander is an **amphibian**. There are about 350 species of salamander, including newts. They are found in many parts of the world. Some live most of their life on land and others in water, but they all breed in or near water. Most are small, but the largest, the giant salamanders, can reach 2.3 metres in length. Giant salamanders lived in the **Miocene Epoch**, and three species are still found today, in China and Japan.

Saltasaurus *noun*
Saltasaurus was the first known **sauropod**. It was about 12 metres long. It had a long tail which may have supported its body on its back legs as it reached up to eat.

Saltopus *noun*
Saltopus was one of the first **dinosaurs** to be discovered, in 1910. It belonged to the **coelurosaur** group, and lived in the **Triassic Period**. It was about 60 centimetres long and ran about on its long hind legs. *Saltopus* probably fed on smaller reptiles and on invertebrates.

Samotherium *noun*
Samotherium was a giraffe which lived in the **Miocene Epoch**, in Europe, Asia and Africa. It was about three metres long, and was more like an okapi than a giraffe in shape, with a relatively short neck. Unlike living giraffes, *Samotherium* probably grazed on open grassland, like an antelope.

sandstone *noun*
Sandstone is a kind of **sedimentary rock**. It is made of sand grains glued together by chemical cement. Sandstone is soft and easy to cut and shape. When animals became buried in sand, their **fossils** were sometimes preserved in sandstone.

sarcopterygian *noun*
A sarcopterygian, or lobe-finned **fish**, is one of a group of bony fish. It has thick, limb-like fins. The sarcopterygians include the lungfish and the **coelacanth**. **Fossils** of these fish first appeared in the **Devonian Period**. The first **amphibians** probably evolved from the sarcoptergyians. The other group of fish is the **actinopterygians**.

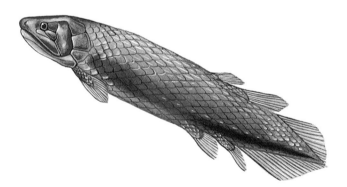

saurischian *noun*
A saurischian is one of a group of **dinosaurs**. The saurischians are the lizard-hipped dinosaurs. The other group is the **ornithischians**, or bird-hipped dinosaurs. In the saurischians, the **hip** bones are like those of normal **reptiles**. Saurischians include **theropods**, which were meat-eating dinosaurs, and **sauropods**, which were plant-eaters.

Saurolophus *noun*
Saurolophus was a duck-billed dinosaur, or
hadrosaur, from the **Cretaceous Period**. Its
fossils have been found in Asia and North
America. *Saurolophus* had a wide head with
a bony crest pointing backwards. It grew to
about nine metres long.

sauropod *noun*
A sauropod was one of a group of
dinosaurs which lived in the **Jurassic** and
Cretaceous Periods. This group includes
the huge, long-necked **herbivores** such as
Brachiosaurus and *Diplodocus*.
Sauropods had a heavy body and a long
neck and tail. They were so big that they
needed to eat huge amounts of vegetation.

sauropodomorph *noun*
A sauropodomorph was a member of a
group of **herbivorous dinosaurs**. It
belonged to the lizard-hipped group, or
saurischians, and lived in the **Triassic**,
Jurassic and **Cretaceous Periods**. The
sauropodomorphs include the **sauropods**
and the **prosauropods**.

Scelidosaurus *noun*
Scelidosaurus was a **dinosaur** which lived
in the **Jurassic Period**. It was about four
metres long and was covered with armour
plates for protection. It also had several rows
of cone-shaped body studs along its back.
Scientists are not sure to which group
Scelidosaurus belongs. It may be related to
the **ankylosaurs**, **stegosaurs** or
ornithopods.

Scutellosaurus *noun*
Scutellosaurus was a small **dinosaur** which
lived in the **Jurassic Period**, in North
America. It belonged to the **ornithopod**
group. It was about 1.5 metres long, of
which about half was its tail. *Scutellosaurus*
had an armoured back which made it
different from most of its relatives.

sea anemone *noun*
A sea anemone is an invertebrate animal.
It lives in the sea and looks like a flower. Sea
anemones have a ring of tentacles around
their mouth. They use their tentacles to
catch small animals to eat. Special cells on
the tentacles paralyse their prey. Sea
anemones can also feed on larger animals
such as crabs and fish. Most adult sea
anemones live attached to rocks and do not
move through the water. Some species can
swim. Sea anemones first appeared in the
sea during the **Silurian Period**.

sea lily ▶ **crinoid**

sea scorpion ▶ **eurypterid**

Secernosaurus *noun*
Secernosaurus was a duck-billed dinosaur,
or **hadrosaur**, which lived in South America,
in the **Cretaceous Period**. It was about
three metres long and fed on plants.

sediment *noun*
Sediment is the solid which settles out from
a river, lake or sea. Stones and mud gather
as sediment at the bottom of rivers, streams
and on the sea-bed. When dead animals
settle in the sediment, they may become
fossilized.

sedimentary rock *noun*
Sedimentary rock is a type of **rock** formed
from **sediments**. One of the most common
sedimentary rocks is **limestone**. It is formed
from the shells of tiny animals. Some
sedimentary rocks contain good examples
of **fossils**.

seed *noun*
A seed is a structure which **plants** make when they reproduce. The seed contains the fertilized ovule, which grows into the **embryo** of a new plant. When the conditions are right, the seed germinates and begins to sprout. Each seed has a store of food, to feed the seedling as it grows. Some seeds are light and blow about. Others have wings to twirl in the wind. Yet others are inside fleshy fruits. Sometimes, seeds are preserved as **fossils**.

seedfern *noun*
A seedfern, or pteridosperm, is an extinct plant with fern-like leaves. The seedferns were not ferns, but belonged to the **gymnosperm** group. The seedferns first appeared in the late **Devonian Period**, and were common in the **Carboniferous Period**.

segnosaur *noun*
A segnosaur was one of a group of **carnivorous dinosaurs**. Skeletons of segnosaurs have been found in Mongolia, and they lived in the **Cretaceous Period**. They may have had an **amphibious** lifestyle and fed on fish. The segnosaurs show some features of the **saurischians** and some features of the **ornithischians**.

Selaginella *noun*
Selaginella is a kind of **club moss**. It belongs to the **pteridophyte** group. Selaginella first appeared in the **Devonian Period** and many species are still found today. Selaginella looks like a moss, and has small, sharp leaves arranged in spirals. It reproduces by means of **spores**.

Sequoia *noun*
Sequoia is a kind of **coniferous tree**, known as redwood. It is a very tall tree which reaches up to 70 metres high. *Sequoia* grows today in the north-west of North America. **Fossils** of *Sequoia* date from as early as the **Jurassic Period**.

serpulid *noun*
A serpulid is a kind of worm. It is an **annelid**, in the same family as lugworms. Serpulids make chalky cases in which they live safe from predators. They can be seen on rocks at the seashore. Serpulid **fossils** date from the **Silurian Period** onwards.

serrated *adjective*
Serrated describes something which is shaped like the teeth of a saw. Some **carnivorous** animals, including several **dinosaurs**, had serrated teeth. These helped the animals to cut up meat.

shale *noun*
Shale is a kind of **sedimentary rock**. It is brittle and breaks easily. Shale is formed when clay and **silt deposits** are turned into rock. Many well-preserved **fossils** have been discovered in beds of shale.

Shantungosaurus *noun*
Shantungosaurus was the largest of the duck-billed dinosaurs, or **hadrosaurs**. Its fossils come from China, from the **Cretaceous Period**. *Shantungosaurus* grew to about 15 metres in length.

shell *noun*

A shell is a hard skeleton on the outside of an **invertebrate** animal. Shells are made of non-living substances such as calcium carbonate and **silica**. Shells support and protect the animal inside them. Many **molluscs** have shells, and these may be paired, as in the **bivalves**, or single, as in the **gastropods**. The **brachiopods** are a fossil group with shells.

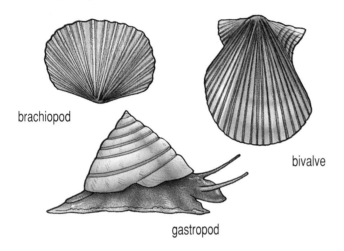

brachiopod

bivalve

gastropod

silica *noun*

Silica is the main chemical in the Earth's crust. It is made of silicon and oxygen. Quartz, flint and opal are all forms of silica. Silica is used to make glass and cement. Silica may preserve **fossils**, and sometimes enters them from volcanic ash.

silt *noun*

Silt is a fine, dust-like substance. It is made of tiny particles of rock. Rivers and streams carry silt, which then settles out on the river bed. Silt sometimes builds up in reservoirs. Silt entering the sea from rivers damages the growth of coral reefs.

Silurian Period ▶ page 134

Silvisaurus *noun*

Silvisaurus was a kind of **reptile** called a nodosaurid. This meant that it was a lumpy, or nodular, reptile. *Silvisaurus* lived in the early **Cretaceous Period**. It grew to about 2.5 metres long.

single-celled creature ▶ **protist**

Sivapithecus *noun*

Sivapithecus was a **mammal** which lived in the **Miocene Epoch**. Like *Ramapithecus* and *Proconsul*, it belonged to the **hominoid** group of primates. *Sivapithecus* was about 1.2 metres tall, and its fossils have been found in Asia. *Sivapithecus* was similar to the orang-utan in some ways.

Sivatherium *noun*

Sivatherium was a large, hoofed **mammal** which lived in the **Pliocene** and **Pleistocene Epochs**. It was related to giraffes, but had spreading antlers, like a moose. Its body was large and heavy and was covered with long, thick fur.

skeleton ▶ page 136

skull *noun*

A skull is part of a **skeleton**. It is the hard, bony structure which surrounds the **brain** of **vertebrate** animals. The skull also protects the eyes, and supports the jawbone. Skulls are often found preserved as **fossils**.

Smilodon *noun*

Smilodon was a sabre-toothed cat, or **machairodont**. It lived in South America during the **Pleistocene Epoch**. *Smilodon* had very long upper canine teeth which reached a length of about 15 centimetres. It used these teeth to stab its prey. *Smilodon* was about two metres long and fed on thick-skinned herbivores.

Silurian Period *noun*

The Silurian Period was a time in **geological history**. The Silurian Period lasted from about 438 million years ago to about 408 million years ago. **Eurypterids** lived in the sea, and the first jawed fish appeared. Many fish had bony armour-plating for protection. The first land plants evolved during the Silurian Period. These included **pteridophytes**.

1. lichen
2. *Cephalaspis*
3. *Poleumita*
4. coral

5. graptolite
6. *Climatius*
7. nautiloid
8. *Cooksonia*

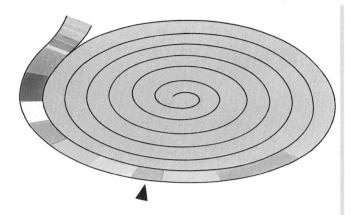

The arrow shows where the Silurian Period lies in relation to the geological history of the Earth.

snake *noun*
A snake is a **reptile**. There are nearly 2,400 species of snake, found in all countries. Snakes have a long, narrow body without any limbs. They range in size from just a few centimetres to 12 metres long. About 300 species of snake are poisonous. Most snakes eat other animals such as small mammals, birds and eggs. Snakes evolved from **lizards**, in the **Cretaceous Period**.

species (plural **species**)   *noun*
A species is a group of living things. Members of the same species can breed together and produce fertile offspring. The species is the basic group in the scientific classification system. Each species is given a double Latin name. The first part of the name is the **genus**, and both names together indicate the species. Many species are now **extinct**, and we only know about them from their **fossils**.

sphenopsid ▶ **horsetail**

spider *noun*
A spider is an **arthropod**. Spiders, and their relatives the scorpions, ticks and mites, belong to the group called arachnids. This group contains about 74,000 species. Spiders have a rounded body, and four pairs of jointed legs. They also have strong jaws with fangs, and some spiders have a poisonous bite. Spiders do not make good **fossils**, so little is known about their history. They probably first appeared in the **Devonian Period**. Spiders have been found preserved in **amber**, from the **Tertiary Period**.

Spinosaurus *noun*
Spinosaurus was a **carnivorous dinosaur**. It lived in the **Cretaceous Period**, in Africa. Like the sail-backed reptiles, or **pelycosaurs**, it had a sail-like flap of skin on its back. *Spinosaurus* was about 15 metres long and had powerful jaws with sharp teeth.

sponge *noun*
A sponge is a soft-bodied **invertebrate** animal. There are about 10,000 species of sponge, and most of these live in the sea. Unlike most animals, adult sponges live fixed in one spot. Their young, or larvae, swim and float in the sea. Sponges feed by filtering tiny pieces of food from the water. They have a spiky skeleton which supports their body. Sponges first appeared in the **Cambrian Period**.

spore *noun*
A spore is a small reproductive body which breaks away from the parent and grows into a new organism. Spores are produced by some **plants**, including fungi, algae, mosses and ferns, as well as by **bacteria** and protozoa. They are often produced in very great numbers and are spread long distances by wind, water or animals.

Spriggina *noun*
Spriggina is an extinct **invertebrate**. It grew to about seven centimetres long and was segmented like a worm. Scientists are not sure what group *Spriggina* belonged to. It lived in the sea, in shallow, sandy areas. Fossils of *Spriggina* date from the **Precambrian Period**.

Stagonolepis *noun*
Stagonolepis was a **reptile** which lived in the **Triassic Period**. It belonged to the **thecodont** group. Unlike most thecodonts, *Stagonolepis* was a **herbivore**. It was about three metres long and looked a little like a short-nosed crocodile. Its body was armoured by heavy plates.

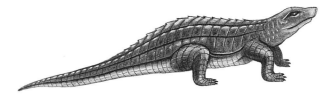

skeleton *noun*

A skeleton is a framework of bones. It supports the body of an animal. A skeleton protects the soft parts of the body, and allows the animal's muscles to work. Many **invertebrate** animals have skeletons called exoskeletons on the outside of their bodies. Other animals have internal skeletons, or endoskeletons. All **vertebrate** animals have endoskeletons. Some of the bones of endoskeletons are jointed. Skeletons are often the parts of the animals which are best preserved as **fossils**.

The backbone protects the spinal cord. It is made up of many small bones, called vertebrae.

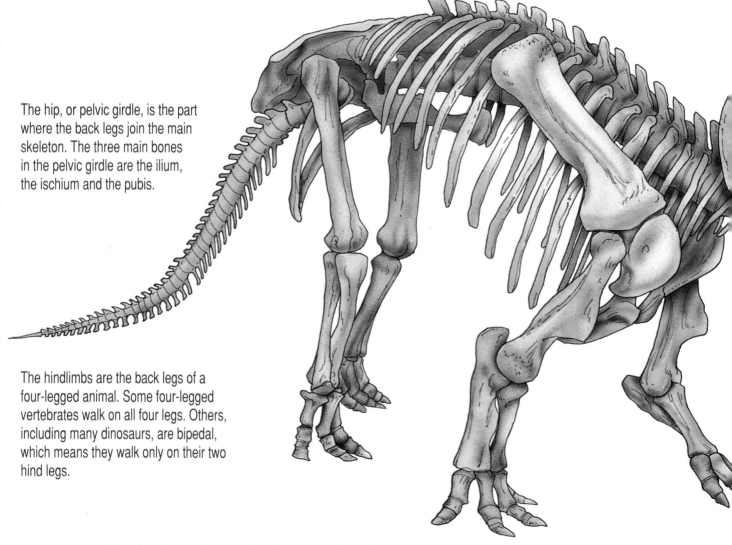

The hip, or pelvic girdle, is the part where the back legs join the main skeleton. The three main bones in the pelvic girdle are the ilium, the ischium and the pubis.

The hindlimbs are the back legs of a four-legged animal. Some four-legged vertebrates walk on all four legs. Others, including many dinosaurs, are bipedal, which means they walk only on their two hind legs.

A claw is a sharp nail on the foot of an animal. Many birds, reptiles, mammals and amphibians have claws, and so do many insects and crustaceans.

The forelimbs are the front legs of a four-legged animal. Many animals use their forelimbs as legs for running. In pterosaurs, birds and bats, the forelimbs are wings.

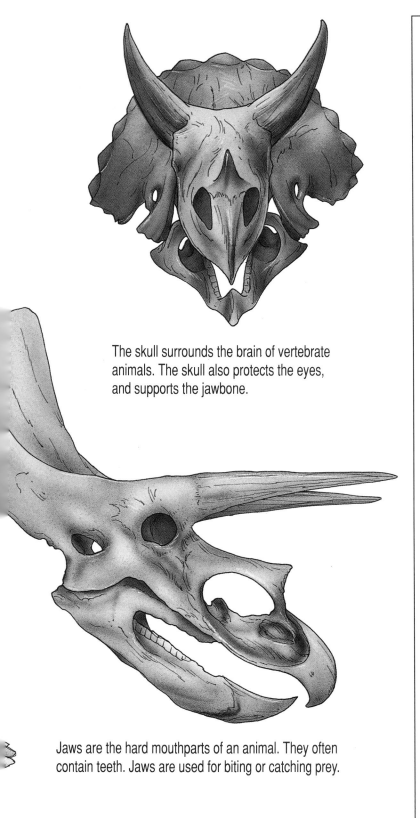

The skull surrounds the brain of vertebrate animals. The skull also protects the eyes, and supports the jawbone.

Jaws are the hard mouthparts of an animal. They often contain teeth. Jaws are used for biting or catching prey.

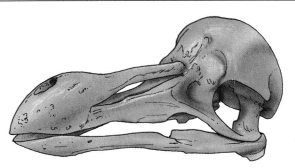

The beak is usually part of the jaw. In bivalve molluscs, the beak is part of the shell.

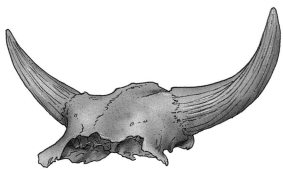

A horn sticks out from an animal's head. Many dinosaurs had horns. Horns are usually made of bone, but the horn of the rhinoceros is made of tightly packed hair.

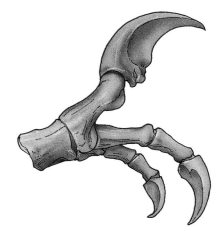

A talon is a long, curved claw used for grasping prey. Many kinds of dinosaur had sharp, curved talons. They used these for attacking their prey, and for holding on to their food. Many birds, especially birds of prey, also have talons.

Staurikosaurus *noun*
Staurikosaurus was a two-legged **dinosaur** from the **Triassic Period**. Its fossils have been found in South America.
Staurikosaurus was about two metres long and fed on smaller animals.

Stegoceras *noun*
Stegoceras was a **herbivorous dinosaur** from the **Cretaceous Period**. It belonged to the **pachycephalosaur** group, and reached about 2.5 metres in length. Its fossils come from North America.

stegosaur *noun*
A stegosaur was one of a group of **dinosaurs** which lived mainly in the **Jurassic Period**. Stegosaurs all had a heavy body and armoured plates or spikes along their back and tail. They were **herbivores**. Examples of stegosaurs are *Stegosaurus* itself, and *Kentrosaurus*.

Stegosaurus *noun*
Stegosaurus is one of the best known of all **dinosaurs**. Its fossils have been found in North America and Europe, and it lived in the **Jurassic Period**. *Stegosaurus* was about nine metres long and had a bridge-shaped body, with large, bony plates along its back. It also had spines on its tail, for defence. The plates on *Stegosaurus's* back may have been for protection, or to control its body temperature. *Stegosaurus* had a very small head and brain for its body size.

stemless palm ► Nipa

Stenopterygius *noun*
Stenopterygius was an ichthyosaur which lived in the Jurassic Period. We know a lot about the body of *Stenopterygius* because very complete fossils have been found. It was shaped like a dolphin with a fin on its back and a fish-like tail. The front limbs were like flippers, and the hind limbs like short fins. *Stenopterygius* grew to about two metres long and swam fast in the sea. It fed on fish and belemnites.

Stonehenge *noun*
Stonehenge is a large circle of stones, or **megaliths**, in southern England. It was built around 1500 BC. Stonehenge is made up of five separate arches, each built from three huge stones. These are surrounded by a circle of similar arches, joined together.

stratigraphy *noun*
Stratigraphy is the scientific study of **rock** layers, or strata. It involves studying the origin of rocks, what they are made of and where they are found.

stromatolite *noun*
A stromatolite is a **fossil** left behind by some **blue-green alga**. Stromatolites are cylindrical fossils, formed from layers of **limestone**.

Strophomena *noun*
Strophomena was an **invertebrate** animal. It was a **brachiopod** which lived in the **Ordovician Period**. Its fan-shaped shell was about three centimetres long.

Struthiomimus   *noun*
Struthiomimus was a bird-like **dinosaur** from the **Cretaceous Period**. It belonged to the **ornithomimosaur** group. It was about four metres long, with long back legs and small front legs. *Struthiomimus* had a horny beak, like that of a bird.

Styracosaurus   *noun*
Styracosaurus was a horned **dinosaur** which lived in the **Cretaceous Period**. It belonged to the **ceratopsian** group. *Styracosaurus* was about six metres long and was a heavily built **herbivore**. It had a horn on its nose and a neck frill with six long spines.

super-continent ▶ page 140

Supersaurus   *noun*
Supersaurus is one of the largest **dinosaurs** known. It was like *Diplodocus* but even bigger, with a body up to 30 metres in length. Even the shoulder blade of *Supersaurus* is taller than a person. Bones of *Supersaurus* come from a quarry in Colorado, United States of America.

swamp   *noun*
A swamp is a kind of wetland. In a swamp, the water level is high so that the plants growing in it are always waterlogged. In the **Carboniferous Period**, there were many plants specially adapted to growing in swamps.

swamp cypress   *noun*
A swamp cypress is a tree which grows to 30 metres tall. It is a **conifer** which grows in China and is also known as *Metasequoia*. Before it was found alive, the swamp cypress was known only from **fossils**. It is an example of a **living fossil**. Its fossilized remains have been found dating from the **Cretaceous Period**.

synapsid   *noun*
A synapsid was one of a group of **reptiles**. The synapsids are the mammal-like reptiles and include the **pelycosaurs**, the **therapsids** and the **therosaurs**. They first appeared during the **Carboniferous Period** and were most numerous in the **Permian Period**. The synapsids became extinct in the **Jurassic Period**. **Mammals** evolved from the synapsids. The other main reptile groups are the **anapsids**, the **diapsids** and the **euryapsids**.

Syntarsus   *noun*
Syntarsus was a small **dinosaur** which lived in the **Triassic Period**. It was about three metres long and looked like *Coelophysis*. Fossils of *Syntarsus* have been found in Africa.

Synthetoceras   *noun*
Synthetoceras was a hoofed **mammal** which lived in the **Miocene** and **Pliocene Epochs**. It looked rather like a deer, but its strangest feature was that it had a two-pronged horn on its nose as well as a pair of horns on its head.

super-continent *noun*

A super-continent describes one of the huge continents that existed early in the history of the Earth. The continents of today may once have been joined together in a single super-continent called **Pangaea**. **Gondwana** and **Laurasia** were two super-continents that formed when Pangaea split apart during the Mesozoic Era. They later split again to create the continents of today. Scientists believe the continents of the world are still moving very, very slowly.

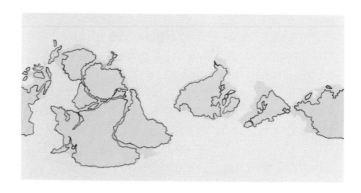

1. During the early Cambrian Period, North America, Europe and Asia were all near the Equator.

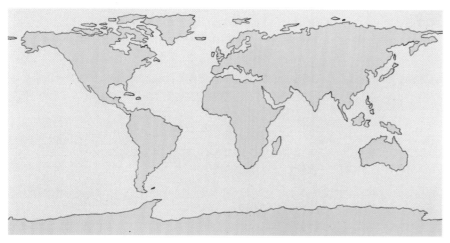

7. In the present day, India is joined to the rest of Asia, and Australia has split off from Antarctica.

The striped areas indicate shallow seas.

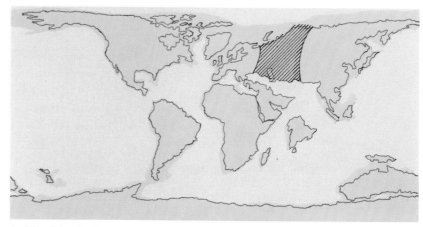

6. The Atlantic Ocean opened up in the Paleocene Epoch. South America and Australia were still connected to Antarctica.

2. North America and Europe were joined in the Silurian Period, with the other continents linked together.

3. During the mid-Carboniferous Period, the continents moved towards each other.

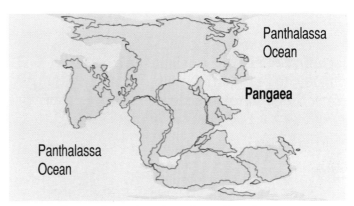

4. The continents fused together to form Pangaea.

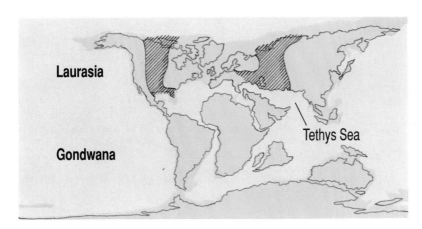

5. Pangaea broke up during the mid-Cretaceous Period, to form Gondwana and Laurasia.

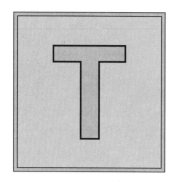

Taeniolabalis *noun*
Taeniolabalis was a small **mammal** which lived in the **Paleocene Epoch**. It was about 60 centimetres long and looked like a rodent. Its fossils have been found in Mongolia and in North America. *Taeniolabalis* lived in tropical forests. It had special, flat teeth for grinding its food.

tail *noun*
A tail is a thin extension of the **backbone** in **vertebrate** animals. Many animals have a long tail, to help them balance, climb or swim. Some **dinosaurs**, such as the **ankylosaurs**, used their armoured tails for protection.

talon *noun*
A talon is the claw of an animal. It is a long, curved claw used for grasping prey. Many kinds of **dinosaur** had sharp, curved talons. They used these for attacking their prey, and for holding on to their food. Many **birds**, especially birds of prey, also have talons.

taphonomy *noun*
Taphonomy is the study of how the environment affects the remains of animals and plants after they have died. It includes the processes involved in **fossilization**.

tar pit *noun*
A tar pit is a low-lying area filled with a natural **deposit** of tar. Tar is a black, sticky substance. It is formed when coal is heated without air. Sometimes, animals have become trapped in tar pits, and their bodies have been preserved.

Tasmanian wolf ► **thylacine**

taxonomy *noun*
Taxonomy is the practice of naming and classifying animals and plants.

teeth ► page 144

Teloceros *noun*
Teloceros was a hoofed **mammal** which lived in the **Miocene Epoch**. It was related to the rhinoceros but lived an **amphibious** life, like a hippopotamus.

tentacle *noun*
A tentacle is a finger-like part of an **invertebrate's** body. **Sea anemones**, **corals** and many worms have tentacles, as do squids and octopuses. Most animals use their tentacles to catch their food.

Teratornis *noun*
Teratornis was a huge **bird** which lived in South America and North America until a few thousand years ago. It stood about 1.5 metres tall and had a wingspan of about 5 metres. *Teratornis* was a kind of vulture and fed on the carcasses of mammals. Its remains have been found in **tar pits**.

terrestrial reptile ► page 146

Tertiary Period *noun*
The Tertiary Period was a time in **geological history**. It lasted from about 65 million to about 2 million years ago.

Tethys Sea *noun*
The Tethys Sea was an area of water which separated the super-continents of **Laurasia** and **Gondwana**, in the **Mesozoic Era**.

Tetralophodon *noun*
Tetralophodon was an early form of elephant. It lived in Europe, Asia and North America during the **Miocene** and **Pliocene Epochs**. It stood about 2.5 metres high at the shoulder and had a long head. It had tusks which curved downwards from the upper jaw.

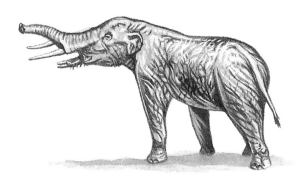

thecodont *noun*
A thecodont was one of a group of **reptiles**. The thecodonts lived in the **Permian** and **Triassic Periods**. They evolved into the **dinosaurs**, **pterosaurs** and **crocodilians**.

therapsid *noun*
A therapsid was a member of a group of **synapsid reptiles**. The therapsids lived from the **Permian** until the early **Jurassic Periods**. They were related to **mammals**.

theria *plural noun*
The theria are one of the two main groups of **mammals**. They are the live-bearing mammals. The theria include **marsupials** and **placental mammals**. They evolved from mammal-like reptiles late in the **Jurassic Period**. The theria became widespread in the **Cenozoic Era**. The other group is the **prototheria**.

theropod *noun*
A theropod was a member of a group of **carnivorous dinosaurs**. The theropods walked on their hind legs and fed on other **dinosaurs**. They included the **coelurosaurs** and the **carnosaurs**. Theropods lived from the **Triassic** to the **Cretaceous Periods**.

therosaur *noun*
A therosaur was one of a group of **synapsid reptiles**. The therosaurs lived in the **Permian** and **Triassic Periods**. They gradually became more and more like mammals.

thick-headed reptile ►
pachycephalosaur

thinking people ► **Homo sapiens**

Thoatherium *noun*
Thoatherium was a small, horse-like **mammal** which lived in South America in the **Miocene Epoch**. It was about one metre long and had a single, hoof-like toe on each foot. *Thoatherium* was not closely related to horses, but evolved separately.

Thrinaxodon *noun*
Thrinaxodon was a mammal-like **reptile** which lived in the **Triassic Period**. Its fossils have been found in South Africa and Antarctica. Thrinaxodon belonged to the **cynodont** group. It looked like a weasel in shape and was about 50 centimetres long.

teeth *plural noun*

Teeth are the hard, bone-like parts that are fixed to the jaws of animals. There are three main types of tooth. The molars are wide flat teeth at the back of the mouth. They are used for chewing food. Incisors are sharp teeth used for chopping food. Canines are sharp, pointed teeth used for biting and tearing. Teeth are often found as **fossils**.

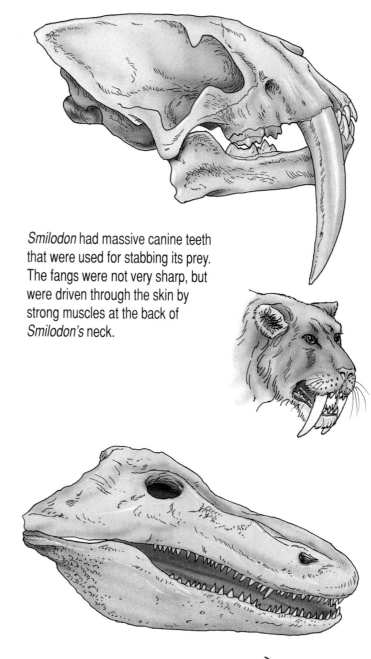

Smilodon had massive canine teeth that were used for stabbing its prey. The fangs were not very sharp, but were driven through the skin by strong muscles at the back of *Smilodon's* neck.

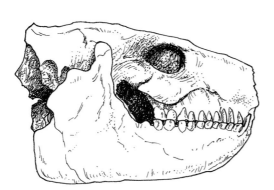

Heterodont teeth

Merycoidodon probably grazed grass. Its well developed canines and incisors show that it probably also ate other food. Teeth that are used for biting, tearing and chewing are known as heterodont teeth.

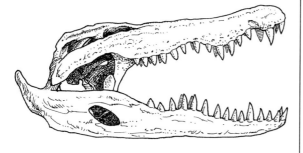

Homodont teeth

A crocodile has sharp teeth that are all of the same kind. The teeth are not good for chewing, but can catch and hold prey. Teeth of a single kind are called homodont teeth.

The sharp teeth of *Eryops* show that it probably caught its prey in the same way as a modern crocodile.

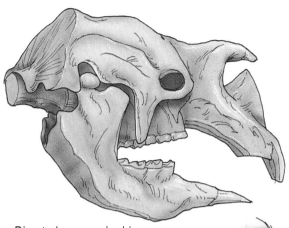

Diprotodon was a herbivorous marsupial. *Diprotodon* had two large incisors, like a beaver's, and flat molars at the back for chewing plant food. Fossils of *Diprotodon* have been found in South Australia.

The woolly mammoth's incisors are long tusks measuring about 4.8 metres. They may have been used to dig for plant food buried under the snow.

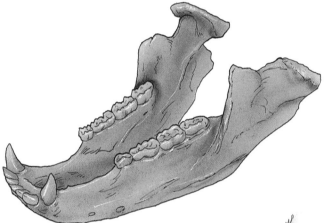

The cave bear had no front molars between the canines and the back molars. In the modern bear, this gap is filled with more molars.

Megazostrodon was very like a modern shrew. It had sharp teeth for eating insects, and could probably move around quickly.

terrestrial dinosaur *noun*

A terrestrial dinosaur was a **dinosaur** that lived on land. Dinosaurs generally had high ankles, and walked on their toes. The legs and feet of terrestrial dinosaurs varied greatly. A large, heavy animal needed broad feet to take its weight. Light animals usually had narrow, bird-like feet.

The skeleton of *Struthiomimus* is very like that of a modern ostrich, and scientists think that it could run just as fast.

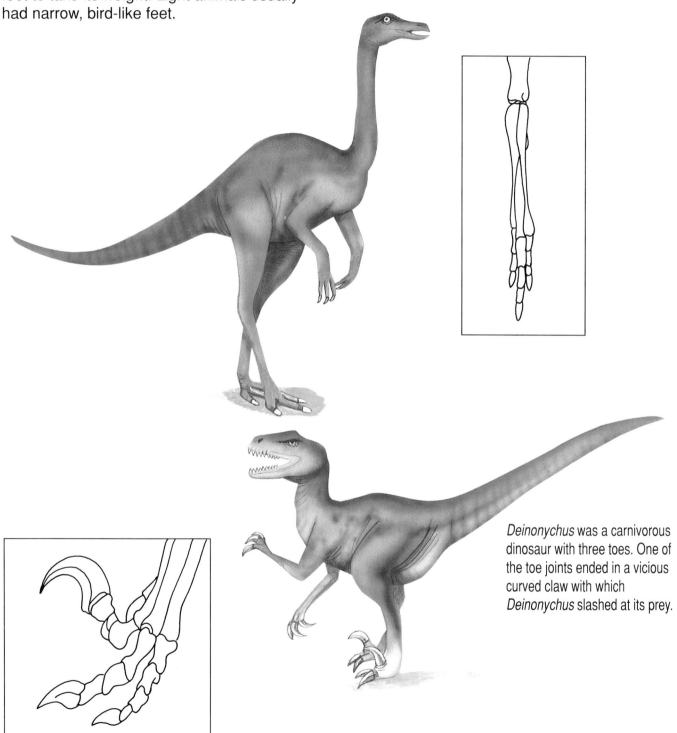

Deinonychus was a carnivorous dinosaur with three toes. One of the toe joints ended in a vicious curved claw with which *Deinonychus* slashed at its prey.

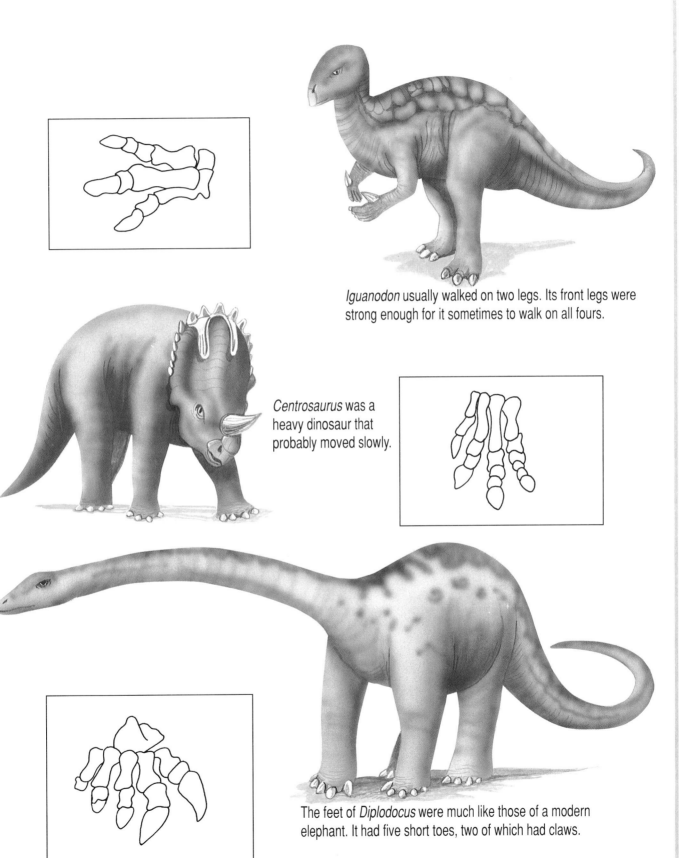

Iguanodon usually walked on two legs. Its front legs were strong enough for it sometimes to walk on all fours.

Centrosaurus was a heavy dinosaur that probably moved slowly.

The feet of *Diplodocus* were much like those of a modern elephant. It had five short toes, two of which had claws.

Thylacoleo   *noun*
Thylacoleo was the **marsupial** lion. It was a lion-like **mammal** which lived in Australia until about 30,000 years ago. *Thylacoleo* fed on marsupial herbivores, using its sharp incisor teeth.

Thylacinus   *noun*
Thylacinus, or the Tasmanian wolf, was a **carnivorous marsupial**. It lived in Tasmania. There are no reliable records of *Thylacinus* being spotted since the 1930s and it is probably now extinct. It was built like a dog, and fed on smaller mammals and birds.

Thylacosmilus   *noun*
Thylacosmilus was a **carnivorous marsupial** which lived in South America, during the **Miocene** and **Pliocene Epochs**. It looked like the sabre-toothed cats, but was not related. Like them, it had very long, dagger-like teeth in its upper jaw. These teeth grew to about 20 centimetres in length. *Thylacosmilus* was about the size and shape of a jaguar.

Ticinosuchus   *noun*
Ticinosuchus was a **reptile** which lived in the **Triassic Period**. It belonged to the **thecodont** group, and looked like a crocodile. *Ticinosuchus* was about three metres long and had a slender body, with a long tail. It had sharp teeth and fed on smaller reptiles. *Ticinosuchus* walked and ran on four legs.

Titanohyrax   *noun*
Titanohyrax was a **mammal**. It was a giant hyrax. *Titanohyrax* lived in the **Oligocene Epoch** in North Africa. It looked like a huge guinea pig, reaching two metres in length. It is the largest hyrax so far discovered.

Titanosaurus   *noun*
Titanosaurus was a **herbivorous dinosaur** which lived in the **Cretaceous Period**. It was a **sauropod**, and grew to about 12 metres long. Its fossils have been found in Asia, Europe, Africa and South America.

tool   *noun*
A tool is an object used by an animal to help it to do something. Some animals, such as chimpanzees, use tools to help them find their food. It is mostly only intelligent animals which use tools. **Humans** gained many advantages over animals when they began using tools.

tool-making   ► page 150

tortoise   *noun*
A tortoise is a hard-shelled **reptile**. Tortoises belong to the **anapsid** group of reptiles. There are about 40 species of tortoise alive today. Tortoises first appeared in the late **Triassic Period**. Their basic shape has changed very little.

Toxodon   *noun*
Toxodon was a **mammal** which lived in South America during the **Pliocene** and **Pleistocene Epochs**. It was about three metres long and had a head like a rhinoceros. Its teeth were more like those of a rodent. *Toxodon* was a **herbivore**.

trace fossil   *noun*
A trace fossil is the fossil made by the activity of an animal. Examples of trace fossils are **footprints**, burrows, tooth marks, **coprolites**, **nests** and **tools**. Trace fossils are mostly found in sandy **sediments**, **mudstones** or **shales**.

tree *noun*

A tree is a large, woody plant with a tall stem, or trunk. Some trees are evergreen, with leaves all year round. Other trees are deciduous, losing their leaves for part of each season. The largest trees live for many hundreds of years and may reach heights of over 100 metres.

tree fern *noun*

A tree fern is one of a group of tropical **ferns**. Tree ferns have a tall, woody stem. The fern fronds grow from the top of this stem. Tree ferns look like **cycads**, but their leaves are more fern-like. Tree ferns were most common in the **Carboniferous Period**, when some reached up to eight metres tall. There are six living **genera** of tree ferns.

Triassic Period ► page 152

Triceratops *noun*

Triceratops is the most familiar of the horned dinosaurs, or **ceratopsids**. It lived in the **Cretaceous Period**. It was very large, reaching about nine metres long. *Triceratops* had a heavy, beak-like mouth and three sharp spikes on its head. A stiff frill protected its neck. About 20 different species of *Triceratops* have been discovered.

triconodont *noun*

A triconodont was one of a group of early **mammals**. It was a small insect-eater but little is known about it since only jaw fossils have been found. It lived in the **Triassic** and **Cretaceous Periods**.

Trigonocarpus *noun*

Trigonocarpus is a seedfern. It lived in the **Carboniferous Period**. The tree of *Trigonocarpus* grew to about five metres in height. It is the seeds which are usually found as fossils. These are oval-shaped and divided by three ribs.

trilobite *noun*

A trilobite was an **invertebrate**. Trilobites lived in the sea from the **Cambrian** to the **Permian Periods**. About 4,000 species of trilobite have been described. Trilobites probably lived in shallow seas and crawled about on the mud. They ranged in size from about one millimetre to about one metre long and had a hard, protective shell. Trilobites had several pairs of jointed legs and many of these legs also had gills, for breathing.

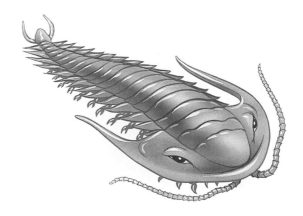

Tsintaosaurus *noun*

Tsintaosaurus was a duck-billed dinosaur, or **hadrosaurid**, from China. It lived in the **Cretaceous Period**. *Tsintaosaurus* was up to 10 metres long and had a tall horn on the top of its head.

tuatara *noun*

A tuatara is a **reptile**. It is only found on certain islands off the north coast of New Zealand. Because it is very similar to fossil reptiles which became extinct 140 million years ago, the tuatara is sometimes called a **living fossil**. Tuataras grow very slowly, and some live to be over 100 years old.

149

tool-making   *noun*

Tool-making refers to the ability of humans to make tools. The first human to use tools was **Homo habilis**. The first tools were made from stone and flint during the Old **Stone Age**, from 600,000 to 10,000 BC. During the Middle and New Stone Age, people gradually learned how to make more sophisticated tools out of different materials. In the **Bronze Age** and **Iron Age**, people started to use metals to make tools.

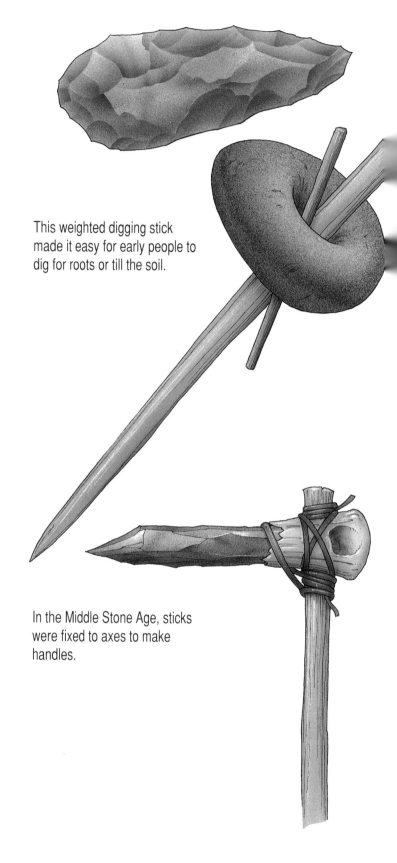

This weighted digging stick made it easy for early people to dig for roots or till the soil.

In the Middle Stone Age, sticks were fixed to axes to make handles.

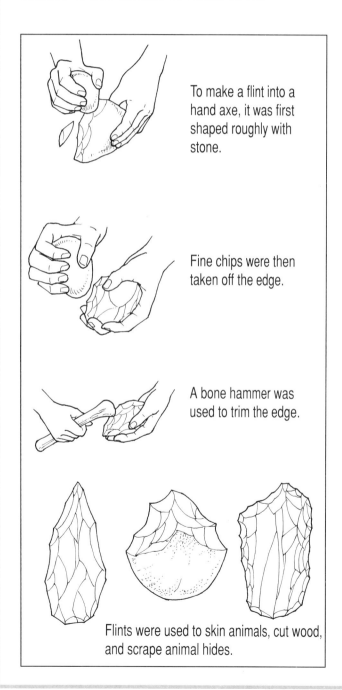

To make a flint into a hand axe, it was first shaped roughly with stone.

Fine chips were then taken off the edge.

A bone hammer was used to trim the edge.

Flints were used to skin animals, cut wood, and scrape animal hides.

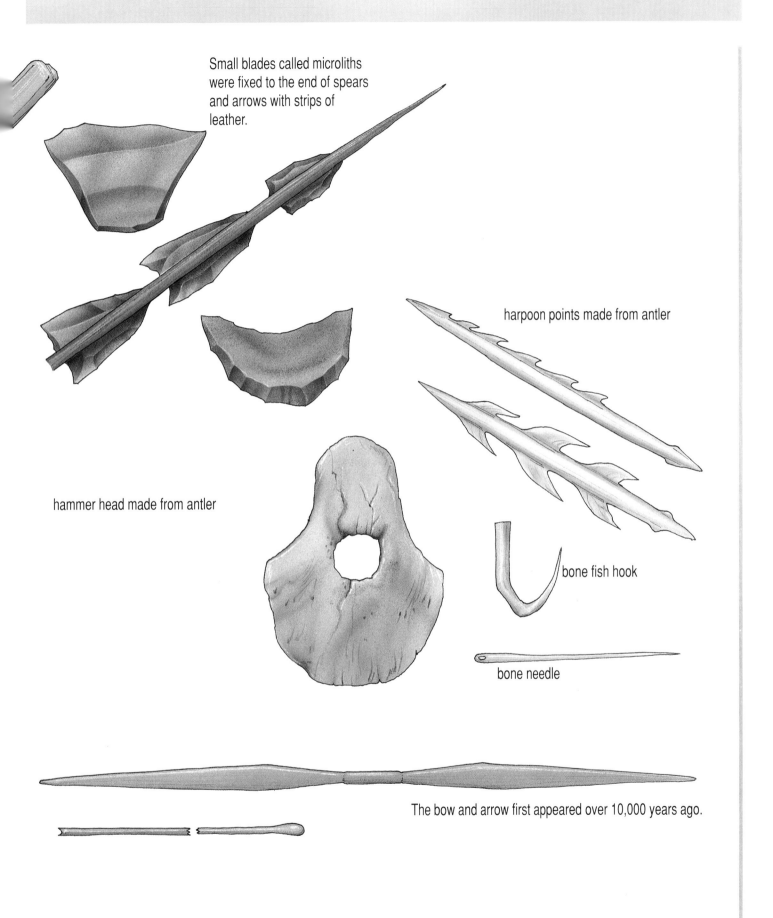

Small blades called microliths were fixed to the end of spears and arrows with strips of leather.

harpoon points made from antler

hammer head made from antler

bone fish hook

bone needle

The bow and arrow first appeared over 10,000 years ago.

Triassic Period   *noun*

The Triassic Period was a time in **geological history**. The Triassic Period lasted from about 248 million years ago to about 213 million years ago. The first **dinosaurs** appeared during the Triassic Period. Carnivorous mammal-like reptiles called cynodonts evolved. There were also many kinds of **aquatic reptile**, including tortoises and turtles. Palm-like cycads grew in the Triassic Period. The tallest cycads grew to about 15 metres.

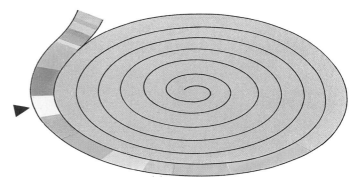

The arrow shows where the Triassic Period lies in relation to the geological history of the Earth.

1. *Thrinaxodon*
2. *Kannemeyria*
3. *Ticinosuchus*
4. *Coelophysis*
5. *Cynognathus*
6. *Saltopus*
7. *Nothosaurus*
8. *Mixosaurus*
9. *Ophthalmosaurus*

tumulus (plural **tumuli**)   *noun*
A tumulus is a kind of earthwork. Tumuli were made by early people as burial mounds. Today's tumuli appear as small hills, with gently sloping sides. Tumuli are usually round or oval in shape.

tundra   *noun*
The tundra is a treeless habitat. There are Arctic and Alpine tundras and the plants growing in them include low shrubs, grasses, mosses and lichens. They support many animals. The Arctic tundra replaces the taiga in the far north of North America, Europe and Asia. Many arctic birds, such as ducks and waders, nest in the tundra. Alpine tundras are the areas on mountains which are too high for trees to grow.

Tylosaurus   *noun*
Tylosaurus was an **aquatic reptile** which lived in the **Cretaceous Period**. It belonged to the same group as **Mosasaurus**. It is related to the monitor lizards of today. *Tylosaurus* was about six metres long, with paddle-like limbs. It hunted other animals in shallow seas.

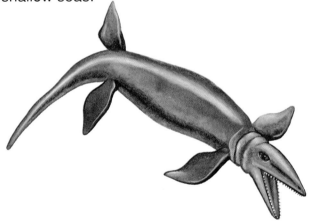

Tyrannosaurus   *noun*
Tyrannosaurus is one of the most famous of all **dinosaurs**. It lived in the **Cretaceous Period**, and its fossils come from North America. *Tyrannosaurus* was one of the largest of the meat-eating **carnosaurs**, and measured up to about 12 metres long. It had a very large head with long, sharp teeth.

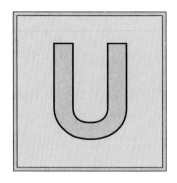

Uintatherium   *noun*
Uintatherium was a **mammal** which lived in the **Eocene Epoch**. It was a large, hoofed mammal. *Uintatherium* looked rather like a rhinoceros. It had six bony horns on its head and also a pair of tusks poking downwards from its top lip.

Ultrasaurus   *noun*
Ultrasaurus was a huge **dinosaur**. It was related to **Brachiosaurus** and **Supersaurus**, but even larger than both. Ultrasaurus lived in the **Jurassic Period** and its bones were found in Colorado in 1979. It may have been over 30 metres long and weighed 130 tonnes. This makes *Ultrasaurus* the largest animal that ever lived on Earth.

ungulate   *noun*
An ungulate is a hoofed **mammal**. There are two groups of ungulates. The odd-toed ungulates include rhinoceroses and horses. The even-toed ungulates include pigs and deer. All ungulates are **herbivores**. They first appeared in the **Eocene Epoch**.

upright people ► **Homo erectus**

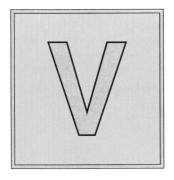

Velociraptor   *noun*
Velociraptor was a **carnivorous dinosaur** which lived in the **Cretaceous Period**. It was about two metres long and had sharp, curved claws on its hind feet. It belonged to the deinonychosaur group.

vertebra (plural **vertebrae**)   *noun*
A vertebra is one of the individual bones which make up the **backbone**. The vertebrae protect the nerves of the spine. They allow movement of the back by rocking slightly against each other. Vertebrae are some of the bones most commonly preserved as fossils.

vertebrate   *adjective*
Vertebrate describes those animals which have a **backbone**. There are seven groups of vertebrate animal. These are jawless fish, cartilaginous fish, bony fish, amphibians, reptiles, birds and mammals. There are about 45,000 species of vertebrate animal. Animals without backbones are known as **invertebrate** animals.

Vulcanodon   *noun*
Vulcanodon was a large **herbivorous dinosaur** from the early **Jurassic Period**. It was a member of the **sauropod** group and lived in southern Africa. *Vulcanodon* had a huge body, long tail and neck, and a very small head. It probably walked on four thick legs. Only a few fossilized bones of *Vulcanodon* have been found, so not much is known about this dinosaur.

worldwide dinosaur discoveries *noun*

Many worldwide dinosaur discoveries have been made in the last 200 years. The first fossil dinosaurs were identified in the early 1800s. Since then, **paleontologists** have discovered more and more about dinosaurs. Dinosaur remains have been found on all the modern continents. There may be other fossils in sites that have not yet been excavated.

Europe
The term 'dinosaur' was first used in 1841 by a British scientist, Richard Owen. Most of the finds made in Europe have not been in very good condition.

Iguanodon

North America
Many important dinosaur remains have been found in the western United States of America and Canada.

Deinonychus

South America
The main finds have been in southern Brazil and Argentina.

Saltasaurus

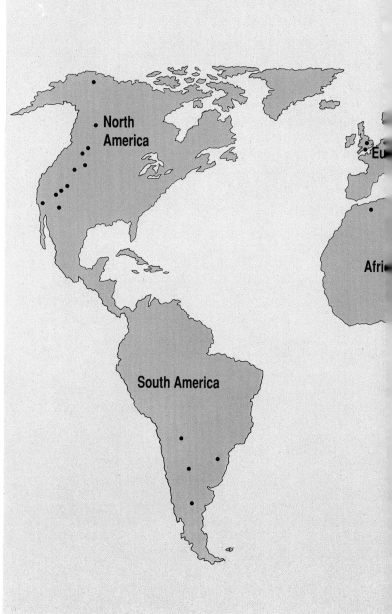

156

Africa

The remains of the oldest dinosaurs have been found in the south of the continent. The most famous excavation site is at Tendaguru, Tanzania.

Brachiosaurus

Lesothosaurus

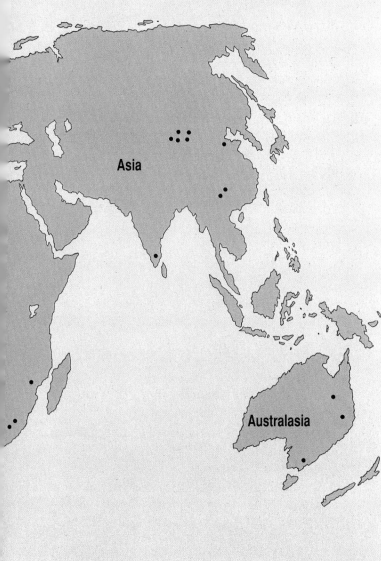

Asia

China has produced some remarkable finds. Many interesting remains have also been found in the Gobi Desert in Mongolia.

Proceratops

Australasia

Many of the discoveries have been made only recently. Dinosaur remains were first found in New Zealand in 1980.

Minmi

Walchia *noun*
Walchia is an extinct plant. It was one of the earliest known **conifers**, and grew in the **Carboniferous Period**. It was similar to the *Cordaites*, but had cones. The cones of Walchia were about eight centimetres long.

warm-blooded *adjective*
Warm-blooded describes those animals which can control their own body temperature. The opposite of warm-blooded is **cold-blooded**. **Birds** and **mammals** are warm-blooded, but all other animals are cold-blooded. Some scientists think that certain **dinosaurs** may also have been warm-blooded.

water scorpion ▶ **eurypterid**

Weigeltisaurus *noun*
Weigeltisaurus was one of the first of the gliding **reptiles**. It lived in the **Permian Period**, and its fossils come from Europe and Madagascar. *Weigeltisaurus* had long ribs sticking out from each side of its body, with skin stretched between to form wings. It could glide between trees. *Weigeltisaurus* was about 25 centimetres long.

welded lizard ▶ **ankylosaur**

Williamsonia *noun*
Williamsonia was one of a family of **bennettites**. It lived in the **Jurassic** and **Cretaceous Periods**. *Williamsonia* grew to a height of about three metres. It had palm-like leaves and large, star-shaped flowers. *Williamsonia* produced cones.

wing *noun*
A wing is one of two parts of an animal's body which are normally used for flight. Many animals have wings, such as flies, butterflies, bats and birds. The wings of insects are made of flattened parts of their external skeleton, or cuticle. In birds, bats and the extinct **pterosaurs**, the wings are formed from the front limbs. The surface of a bird's wing is mostly feathers, but a bat's wing is made from tightly stretched skin.

wolf *noun*
A wolf is a kind of wild dog. There are two species of true wolf alive today. These are the gray wolf and the red wolf. Wolves were once found in many areas where they are not found today. They feature in some of the cave paintings made by **paleolithic** hunters. The bones of wolves have been found in caves dating from about 40,000 years ago. Wolves became extinct in England around 1500, in Scotland around 1740 and in Ireland around 1770. The largest known wolf was the dire wolf. It was common in western North America during the **Pleistocene Epoch**.

woolly mammoth ▶ **mammoth**

woolly rhinoceros ▶ **Coelodonta**

world dinosaur discoveries ▶ page 156

worm *noun*

A worm is an invertebrate animal with a long, soft body. Worms belong to various groups. Their bodies do not usually preserve well, and so are not often found as fossils. Some worms, such as **serpulids**, make hard tubes which do fossilize.

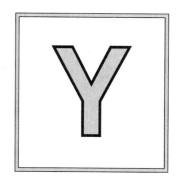

Youngina *noun*

Youngina was a small, lizard-like **reptile** which lived in the **Permian Period**. It was about 30 centimetres long and had a small head with sharp teeth. *Youngina* probably ate insects.

Yunnanosaurus *noun*

Yunnanosaurus was a **dinosaur** which lived in the **Jurassic Period**. It belonged to the **saurischian** group of dinosaurs, known as **prosauropods**. Like the other prosauropods, *Yunnanosaurus* was a **herbivore**.

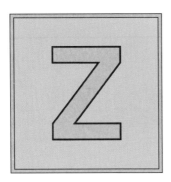

Zalambdalestes   *noun*
Zalambdalestes was an early form of **mammal**. It lived in the **Cretaceous Period**, at around the time of the last **dinosaurs**. *Zalambdalestes* was shrew-like and about 15 centimetres long. It is very similar to many living **insectivores**.

zeuglodont   *noun*
A zeuglodont was an early form of whale. The zeuglodonts lived mainly in the **Eocene Epoch**, in the warmer parts of the **Tethys Sea**. They had a long snout and short hind limbs. The zeuglodonts had **incisor** and **canine** teeth, for feeding on molluscs and crustaceans. By the **Miocene Epoch**, the zeuglodonts had become extinct.

zone   *noun*
A zone is a series of layers, or strata, in rocks. Each zone has its own collection of **fossils**.

Zosterophyllum   *noun*
Zosterophyllum was one of the earliest land **plants**. It grew near the edges of lakes in the **Silurian** and **Devonian Periods**. It was a simple plant, about 25 centimetres tall, and reproduced by **spores**. It probably evolved into the tall club mosses of the **Carboniferous Period**, such as *Lepidodendron*.